BREAKING
NEW
GROUND

The First
SCOTTISH
ECUMENICAL
ASSEMBLY
2001

BREAKING
NEW
GROUND

SCOTTISH ECUMENICAL ASSEMBLY 2001

ISBN 0 86153 400 X

All copy keyed by Action of Churches Together in Scotland
Typeset in Gill Sans Light and Van Dijck
Cover design and logo by
The Church of Scotland Department of Design
All other graphics thanks to Nicholas Mynheer
Printed and bound in Great Britain by Mackays

This book was produced in collaboration with Mainstream Publishing
to whom sincere thanks is conveyed

CONTENTS

PREFACE

BREAKING NEW GROUND ...

This is the challenging theme for the first ever Scottish Ecumenical Assembly.

From early reflections in the ACTS Unity, Faith and Order Commission, reinforced by the words of Cardinal Winning when he was invited to address the General Assembly of the Church of Scotland in 1995,

> My vision looks to the day when the entire Christian family in
> Scotland will gather together in Assembly such as this . . .

ACTS Central Council has actively prepared for the first Scottish Ecumenical Assembly in September 2001. The ACTS Implementation Group has co-ordinated the production of this ground-breaking publication and we are grateful to them for providing us with an invaluable aid to help prepare us for our encounters in September.

We are indebted to the nine writers of this book for sharing their expertise and for inspiring and challenging us in our study of the seven themes chosen for our reflection, exploration and discovery together. The prime purpose of the Assembly is to make broad policy together as Churches in Scotland committed to each other in Christ. The policy emerging should be seen to affect the future of the whole of Scotland – and so our sub-theme is . . . a renewed Church in a renewed Nation for a new century.

Others who read this book may not be attending the Assembly. My hope is that they too will find insight and prophetic challenge in the chapters and so feel part of the journey into the future Scotland that those in the Assembly take together. ACTS is about the 'Action of Churches Together in Scotland' and the Assembly aims to create an atmosphere of mutual trust and goodwill which will produce agreed action towards the Ecumenical Vision to which we all aspire in Christ.

We live in exciting times and I am delighted to welcome this book of themes for our historic first Ecumenical Assembly. Let us pray as we prepare together so that we may be renewed in faith, and witness to and unleash the vitality and life giving power of the Spirit of God in the Church and in our nation.

Sister Maire Gallagher CBE SND
Convener, ACTS Central Council
April 2001

INTRODUCTION

Breaking New Ground – a renewed Church in a renewed Nation for a new century.

'Hear what the Spirit is saying to the churches!' is the repeated plea that runs through the opening chapters of the biblical Revelation of John. Seven churches are addressed in a style that blends prophecy with apocalyptic vision. This book of themes for the Scottish Ecumenical Assembly has seven chapters and while none of our writers would lay claim to being 'a prophet' there is, nevertheless, a belief on our part that they have something prophetic to say to the churches and the nation at the start of a new millennium.

The Assembly's seven themes emerged through a process of synthesis. We began with a far wider draft of possibilities and then honed the list to this final selection. Uppermost in our minds throughout was the imperative of 'mission'. A central tenet of ACTS is 'action' and so we sought to offer themes that had potential to create challenge and change in the way the churches consider and make effective their mission. We affirm that while mission is clearly implied in the theme 'Dynamic Ways of Being Church', it is also very much to the fore in themes dealing with Poverty, Alienation and Work. Indeed, the writer of the chapter on Poverty calls for a sea-change in attitude and alignment among Scotland's churches so that we may identify more clearly with the poor in our midst as well as overseas. Clearly, in a Scotland that has become multi-faith and multi-racial, Alienation becomes an essential issue of Christian mission.

The challenges of mission are also to the fore in two other themes, those of Enlightenment and Science and Technology. While often misunderstood or over-emphasised in importance, 'The Enlightenment' had huge influence on a whole range of creative drives that led Scotland to be at the forefront of thought, literature and invention in past centuries. While a 'New Enlightenment' cannot be made-to-order, it may, nevertheless, be possible to wrestle with hopes and possibilities in the field of Education and so begin to envisage the impetus that 'a New

Enlightenment' could create within Scotland and beyond. And consider also the challenges of mission for churches whose members are daily at the interface of Science and Technology. As a former General Secretary of the World Council of Churches, Dr. Philip Potter, said here in Scotland, 'Everyone does theology: he or she engages in an almost daily process of action, speech and reflection. He or she tries to live out and to see sense in the faith that's professed.' The chapter on 'Partnership with Science and Technology' poses questions, dilemmas and issues of life here and now where men and women are called to be 'little less than God' (Psalm 8) in creative power and decision-making.

Under-girding and making possible both 'discipleship' and 'mission' is our human spirituality. It should come as no surprise that two chapters feature spirituality and church-life, those of 'Breaking through to a Fresh Spirituality' and 'Breaking into Dynamic Ways of Being Church'. It is the way we interpret our 'calling in Christ' and channel our 'love of the Church' that leads Christians to be both 'vessels of the Spirit' and 'servants of Christ'. These chapters feature personal faith and congregations as communities of faith – and both are essential for mission.

A glance at the list of seven themes may raise questions of issues not featured. There is, for example, no separate theme on Women's Issues. It is precisely because we have sought to let women's issues emerge through every theme of the Scottish Ecumenical Assembly that we have not created a specific theme. Other possible themes are likewise absent. It is not within the scope of A.C.T.S. (despite the breadth of its Commissions' work and thinking) nor the scope of the Ecumenical Assembly to tackle an all-embracing agenda. The themes featured describe some, but by no means all, of the issues facing Scotland's churches and people at the start of the 21st century.

One of the tasks of the Assembly will be to produce Statements, pointers for ways forward and work yet to be done that will give the churches renewed focus for 'things they can do both separately and together'. These Statements, we hope, will commend themselves to the churches and also have relevance for the wider society.

Breaking New Ground is both this book's title and the overall theme of the Scottish Ecumenical Assembly. It was Jeremiah whose call was defined in terms of 'breaking down and building up' and Prof. James Dunn of Durham University, the Assembly's guest theologian, will feature this prophet in his preaching at the start of Assembly. The hope is that all in the Assembly, all who read this book and all who have taken part in Lenten Studies on 'Breaking New Ground' will consider themselves soil in the field of Scotland's life that is being ploughed and made ready for planting and harvest.

'Hear what the Spirit is saying to the churches!' While laying no claim to being prophets, it may be that our writers will indeed prove to be prophetic in some of their glimpses and questions. The issues featured demand engagement. They offer no neatly packaged solutions but rather call for struggle and commitment and the discovery of a faith-life that is relevant for Scotland's churches and nation in a new millennium.

If even a few attitudes and aspects of church and national life change over the years as a consequence of this publication and the emergence of the Assembly's Statements, then we may indeed be able to say that we have – in ways small or large – 'heard what the Spirit is saying to the churches!'

The S.E.A. Implementation Group
W. Stuart Drummond (Convener)
Frank Bardgett and Stephen Smyth
April 2001

THE WRITERS

Biographical profiles

MARTIN JOHNSTONE

Martin Johnstone currently works with the Board of National Mission of the Church of Scotland, supporting churches in urban priority areas across Scotland. He was previously employed as a Church of Scotland parish minister in Bellshill, where the local congregations have developed a range of activities in response to the needs of the local community. He is a past convener of the Church of Scotland's Priority Areas Fund. Martin has a keen interest in helping local churches to find new models of working appropriate to their own context and in encouraging people to learn from one another and the wider world church. He is concerned, with others, to help the churches in Scotland to find ways to recognise a commitment to social justice as a key part of their missionary calling.

GORDON GRAHAM

Gordon Graham is Regius Professor of Moral Philosophy at the University of Aberdeen, a Fellow of the Royal Society of Edinburgh and a Lay Reader in the Scottish Episcopal Church. He has held a variety of visiting positions at colleges and universities in the US and Europe. He is the author of ten books and over sixty articles on a wide variety of themes in politics, ethics, aesthetics and religion. His most recent book, *Evil and Christian Ethics*, was published by Cambridge University Press in November 2000. He is currently at work on a book about science, genetics and religion. Gordon Graham is a regular contributor to BBC Radio Scotland for whom he also wrote and presented *The Silicon Society*, a series of programmes about the impact of information technology. He has written for both *The Scotsman* and the *Daily Telegraph*, and frequently lectures to professional groups on ethical issues.

ELIZABETH TEMPLETON

After 10 years lecturing in the Philosophy of Religion in New College, Edinburgh, Elizabeth Templeton has worked for the last twenty years as a freelance theologian, writing, lecturing and broadcasting. She has been involved in Ecumenical Theology at local, national and international levels, with particular recent commitments to educational and inter-faith issues. Currently convener of ACTS Unity, Faith and Order Commission, she believes that theology is a participatory activity of the whole Church, not an elitist exercise.

MUKAMI MCCRUM

Mukami McCrum is the Moderator of the Women's Advisory Group of the World Council of Churches (WCC), and also the Director of Central Council Scotland Racial Equality Council. She was born in Kenya and has lived in Scotland since 1973. Educated in Kenya and Edinburgh, she has a teaching and social science background. Previously she worked as a community worker, a project co-ordinator, and as a trainer and consultant on equal opportunities, race, gender and development issues concerned with refugees and asylum seekers, migrant workers and minority ethnic people. She works for justice, peace and equality, and campaigns against discrimination while promoting education for transforming conflict and building peace for social and political change. Previously she was a commissioner of the WCC Justice and Peace Unit and convener of the Scottish Churches Agency for Racial Justice. She is also a member of the UK Government Race Relations Forum and the Racial Equality Advisory Forum (Scottish Executive).

GERARD W. HUGHES

Gerard W. Hughes, born in Skelmorlie, Ayrshire, is a Jesuit priest. An early interest in ecumenism took him to Germany, 1956-59, to study theology. He has been a teacher, a University chaplain, director of St. Beueno's Jesuit spirituality centre in N. Wales, and he is currently based in Birmingham. He works ecumenically on spirituality with a particular interest in people active in some form of justice and peace work. He works with others in building up ecumenical spirituality networks, organises training courses in prayer accompaniment and retreat-giving, developing a ministry of lay person to lay person within the churches. He is author of *In Search of a Way*; *God of Surprises*; *Walk to Jerusalem*; *God, Where are You?* all published by Darton, Longman & Todd. He has also written *O God, Why?* (Bible Reading Fellowship) and *God of Compassion'* (Hodder and Stoughton).

JOHN W. DYCE

Jack Dyce is Principal of the Scottish United Reformed and Congregational College, Glasgow and is the Education Secretary in Scotland of the United Reformed Church. He is part-time minister in a pastorate in Greenock. He is a graduate in organisational behaviour and in law, and has masters degrees in education. His professional experience until recently was in community-based adult learning and guidance and he has interests in adult education and the labour market. He is a member of the Chartered Institute of Personnel and Development.

JOHN ELDRIDGE

John Eldridge is Professor of Sociology at the University of Glasgow. He has published extensively in the fields of industrial sociology, the sociology of the media and social theory. He currently chairs the Church of Scotland's Society, Religion and Technology project committee and was a contributor to its recent publication, *Engineering Genesis*. He is a member of the Methodist church.

JOHN DRANE AND OLIVE M. FLEMING DRANE

John Drane teaches practical theology in the University of Aberdeen, and has been involved in the ecumenical movement in Scotland and internationally for the last twenty years. His most recent book is *The McDonaldization of the Church* (London: Darton, Longman & Todd 2000). Olive M Fleming Drane has a full-time ministry in the creative arts and is widely known throughout the Scottish churches for her clowning. She is also an adjunct professor of evangelism in the School of Theology at Fuller Seminary, California. Her personal spiritual journey is documented in the book *Clowns, Storytellers and Disciples* (Oxford: BRF, forthcoming). John & Olive frequently work together. In 1999 they presented the Bible readings at the *Anglican Conference on Evangelism* (ACE) and also made a presentation on 'Religion and Spirituality' to the *Theology and Evangelism* conference as a follow-up to ACE in March 2001.

CHAPTER ONE

BREAKING OUT OF POVERTY

Good News for the Socially Excluded?

Martin Johnstone

INTRODUCTION

It would be straightforward to focus only on urban poverty and for the need for renewal in the poorest parts of our cities. After all, the considerable majority of the poorest areas in Scotland can be found in and around our major post-industrial cities.[1] But, as Aram Eisenschitz points out:

> [the] majority of poor live outside the inner areas. The multiplicity of processes that cause poverty are matched by a diversity of poor areas. It must also be remembered that a significant number of the poor are dispersed throughout rural Britain.[2]

As such we will attempt to focus on people who are living in poverty, on some of the reasons why people are poor and on what can be done about it.

It is likely that in the months immediately preceding the *Scottish Ecumenical Assembly* there will have been a General Election in the UK. However, it has been necessary for this chapter to be written prior to any announcement of an election. There is, therefore, no way of knowing either what the outcome of any such election might be or what policies will be included within the various party manifestos, although reasonably educated guesses may be made about both. It will be presumed that New Labour will continue to exercise considerable influence over policy in Scotland – at the very least it will remain the lead party in the Scottish Executive – and that its policy of tackling poverty and social exclusion primarily 'by building a welfare system which encourages people into work, but at the same time supports vulnerable groups'[23] will be continued.

Finally, it would be tempting here to focus upon the poor in Scotland – to think about sorting out the issues in our own back yard. That would, however, be inappropriate for two main reasons: firstly, we cannot afford to ignore the desperate poverty which exists in many parts of our world – to do so would be a denial of our dignity and relatedness as human beings, and secondly; poverty in Scotland and poverty overseas are intrinsically related to one another.

POVERTY IS A GLOBAL ISSUE

If we believe that women and men are made in the image of God, then we must believe that poverty is a blasphemy. Indeed, according to the Brazilian Roman Catholic Bishop Dom Pedro Casaldaliga, it is the 'macro-blasphemy' of our day.[4] It is estimated that one-fifth of humanity – a billion people – are chronically and acutely malnourished at the same time as we spend a trillion dollars – a thousand billion – on weaponry.[5] One in five people on our planet live and die in poverty. 1,300,000,000 people are forced to live on an income of less than one dollar a day.[6] Although these statistics make harsh reading, the reality comes alive in the stories and experiences of those who are forced to live in poverty. Among these *Let Me Tell You*:[7]

> . . . about 14 year old Gopal from Calcutta. He has no idea of his real name or the identity of his parents. He has spent at least five years of his young life scavenging on India's railway stations, too quiet a character to search the trains, or rob travellers as many of the boys do. He earns between half a rupee and five rupees a day. He says that he would rather starve than ask for money.
>
> . . . about Emmanuel, who is 8, and lives with his mother and sister in a shanty town on the outskirts of Peru's capital city Lima. Like so many other families unable to find housing, they have 'invaded' a piece of wasteland to build their one roomed shack of woven matting.
>
> . . . about some children living in extreme poverty in Cameroon. In this village all the children must travel nine kilometres to attend the nearest primary school. In this village there is no access to drinking water, so they must resort to the polluted water that flows next to a slaughter house, and a public dump.
>
> . . . about a woman in North America who has just had her water

cut off. She has several children, one of them a new born baby. She can't wash their laundry. She can't bathe the children or make them anything to drink. It is very hard for them. They are so discouraged.

The experience of people in Scotland and other parts of the Britain living in poverty is part of this wider context of world poverty. While poverty in the UK is largely defined in relative terms (see discussion below), it is often part of the mischief-making of the rich to try to drive a wedge between those who live in poverty in this country and those who live in poverty in other parts of the world. According to the leading sociologist Anthony Giddens:

> . . . [the communities of the socially excluded] are not just pockets of deprivation within national societies, they are fault lines along which the Third World rubs up against the First. . . . The social isolation which separates underprivileged groups from the rest of the social order within nations mirrors the division of rich and poor on a global scale.[8]

The principal factors which cause poverty are consistent throughout the world. This is truer today than ever in the post-industrial global economy in which we live. There is clear evidence that as we have moved from an industrial-based capitalist economy to a post-industrial one, it is the poor who have had to bear the principal burden of this transition. Since the 1970s the inequality between the richest and poorest has grown rapidly. The ratio between the average income of the richest 5% of the world's countries and the poorest 5% increased from 78:1 in 1988 to 123:1 in 1993.[9] And within countries there has been the same growing disparity between the richest and poorest. This has been particularly the case in Britain[10] where the trend towards greater equality evident since the 15th century has been reversed in the last 20 years.[11] According to *Poverty in Scotland (1999)*:

> In the UK between 1979 and 1995/96, the poorest 10% of the population saw their real income fall by 9% [in real terms] after housing costs, while the income of the top tenth rose by 70%.
> In the same period the poorest tenth saw its share of total income drop from 4.0% to 2.2% while the richest 10% saw its share rise from 21% to 27%.[12]

A significant proportion of people in Scotland today are living in poverty. But what do we mean by poverty?

DEFINITIONS OF POVERTY

There is no agreed definition of poverty and how it is to be measured across the political parties in Britain today. The debate continues to be around *absolute poverty*, *relative poverty* and, in recent years, *social exclusion*. It is clear that how we define and measure poverty is largely determined by what we 'intend to do about it'[13] and whose responsibility we think it is.

For example, the Conservative Governments (1979–97) argued that the growth in inequality was an inevitable part of economic life and that it did not, as such, constitute poverty. Policies were targeted at creating wealth in the belief that this wealth would eventually 'trickle down' to the wider population. As we have already noted this did not happen. The Child Poverty Action Group stated at the time:

> Poverty is a term which is rarely heard on the lips of policy-makers . . . The debate . . . has been characterised by bland euphemisms – 'low income,' 'below average income,' 'the bottom ten per cent' – terms which obscure the reality of deprivation, poverty and hardship.[14]

To the extent to which it acknowledged the existence of poor people in Britain, Conservative Government policy during those years was heavily influenced by theories of *dependency culture* and of a growing *underclass* comprising lone parents, criminals and the unemployed who did not want to work for a living.[15] The theory of an *underclass* remains strongly influential in popular thought today. According to Haralambos *et al*:

> Such explanations of poverty remain influential in modern Britain . . . [with] numerous stories in the press about how those living on social security were enjoying comfortable, even extravagant lifestyles at the taxpayer's expense. This type of story continues to feature in the British press.[16]

The New Labour Government, by comparison, has made social inclusion one of the central tenets of its term of office (1997-). It has published Annual Reports on its efforts to tackle poverty and social exclusion[17] and has set ambitious targets[18] (milestones) both at a UK level and (with the Liberal Democrats) at a Scottish level to reduce the numbers of people living in poverty. In these publications the UK Government and the Scottish Executive has used *Half or Below Average Income* (HBAI) indicators to quantify what it has recognised as levels of poverty. In the 2000 Social Justice Report,[19] the Scottish Executive acknowledged the lack of key areas of information and committed itself to the commissioning of further research to give more accurate information about levels of *relative poverty*, particularly in small area and rural communities. It is worth noting that while the Executive is now basing the poverty threshold at 50% of the average annual income the decline, in real terms, of the state benefits system over the last twenty years means that those living on basic benefits are living in poverty. 'Income support . . . is now down to around 20% of average earnings, compared to 30% in the early 1980s'[20] (1998/99 figures).

Although the Scottish Poverty Information Unit has found little evidence for an *underclass*,[21] New Labour has also been heavily influenced by some of the thinking of the New Right and many commentators would be critical of its record in government, especially during the first two years when its 'social security policies [were] largely . . . concerned with a series of actual or proposed cuts in benefits.'[22] Many have also remained suspicious that talk of *social exclusion* has masked an unwillingness on the part of the New Labour Government to address the need for redistributive taxation to tackle effectively the depth of poverty which exists in Britain today. David Byrne writes of:

> . . . the development of the discourse of social exclusion in France in the 1980s as being 'a discourse deliberately chosen for closure, to exclude other potential discourses in European political debate and to depoliticise poverty *as far as income redistribution was concerned*' (Veit-Wilson, *Setting Adequacy Standards*, Policy Press, 1998:97, original emphasis) . . . Certainly the use of 'social exclusion' in the UK in the late 1990s by New Labour seems to be exactly a method of closure in relation to challenges to inequality as a general social issue.[23]

It is hardly surprising, therefore, that in Britain today, there is no single clear-cut definition of poverty. Instead there are definitions for *absolute poverty*, *relative poverty* and *social exclusion*. According to the Scottish Affairs Committee's Report of *Poverty in Scotland*:

> *Absolute poverty* is defined as the lack of sufficient resources with which to keep body and soul together. *Relative poverty* defines

income or resources in relation to the average. It is concerned with the absence of material needs to participate fully in accepted daily life. *Social exclusion* is a new term used by the EU [European Union] and the Government, broadly related to relative poverty. It includes the causes and effects of poverty.[24]

The lack of agreed measurements and definitions of poverty should not overly concern us. It is simply evidence of the differences between the economic and social policies of the main two political parties. Additionally, as the Scottish Poverty Information Unit pointed out in evidence to the Scottish Affairs Committee: 'there [is] no need to become over-concerned with a perfect definition. More important [is] what ultimately [is] done.'[25]

In the ongoing debate about what constitutes poverty, what it does to people, and how it ought to be tackled, all organisations concerned with poverty, including the churches, should seek to ensure that the voices of the poorest are heard. Damian Killeen of the Poverty Alliance pointed out at the 1998 Scottish Poverty Information Unit Conference that: 'Everyone, it seems, is an expert on poverty, except for those who experience it.'[26] Elaine Graham issues a challenge to the churches:

It is necessary to ensure that the voices and perspectives of those most affected by poverty in all its forms are given consideration. This is a fundamental commission of the Church: to counter the invisibility and marginalisation that really constitutes social exclusion.[27]

During the mid-1990s Church Action on Poverty (CAP) organised a number of *Poverty Hearings* where those living in poverty had opportunities to put their case to politicians, church leaders and the wider community.[28] It is important that, working with all those committed to ensuring that the voices of poor people are being clearly heard, such opportunities continue to be given. The task today, in some ways, is more difficult because the Government is once more talking about poverty while some of its policies are apparently condemning vulnerable people to lives of increased hardship and poverty. The insights of poor people will help to ensure that real needs are addressed and that false caricatures are avoided. *Let Me Tell You*:[29]

> . . . what it's like to be the mother of a drug abuser. It means always being afraid for your kids – living in a place where there's no work and nothing to do, and dealers who take advantage of vulnerable young people. . . .It means being pulled in different directions, because the stigma of drugs sticks to all your family.

. . . It means being pulled in different directions as you watch your other kids suffer too. . . .It means wondering, in hospitals, hostels and with the police, at what point your child lost the right to be treated as a human being. . . . My son gave his orange juice to an old man in the hospital because he had no-one to visit him. My son didn't give up caring because he's on drugs. But often it seems, society has.

. . . about my Dad. My mum died a couple of years ago, and my Dad is all alone even though he has five sons and two daughters. Why? Because he says he doesn't need us because he'll fight alone. He says he's going to die soon, just as he was born into the world, in the gutter like most unemployed men who lived and go on living in Glasgow. Being unemployed is the waste of a good man.

. . . that for three years I lived in a damp run-down house. My daughter, who's nearly two had asthma at seven weeks old, and my son who's nearly four, had coughs and colds nearly every week, even in the summer. Four weeks ago, after three years of pestering housing, doctors and MPs, my wish was answered. I moved from twenty three up to four up, and the difference is already showing. I can get up in the morning looking forward to housework and caring for my home instead of worrying that I'm going to get visitors. After three years, the feeling of you've won is great. Keep fighting, one and all.

. . . when you're a child you don't have to think about everyday things that all children take for granted. No need to think about where the money comes from for food, clothes, or bills. But as you grow up, and become a parent, you do nothing but worry about food, clothes and heating. All everyday things have to be paid for, even if it means robbing Peter to pay Paul, or pretending not to be in when the cheque man calls to be paid. Bills accumulate and we worry ourselves sick. Unpaid bills don't kill people, but unemployment and poverty kills a little bit of everybody here, piece by piece, every day.

While there is increasingly broad agreement that the existence of poverty is an issue which affects all of us, there is no denying that those most affected are those who are living in poverty.

VICTIMS OF POVERTY: PLACES AND PEOPLE

According to Michael Pacione, who has written widely on urban and rural deprivation in Scotland:

> Poverty is a key factor underlying multiple deprivation. The root cause of deprivation is economic and stems from two main sources. The first arises due to the low wages earned by those employed in declining traditional industries or engaged, often on a part-time basis, in the newer service-based industries. The second cause is the unemployment experienced by those marginal to the job market such as single parents, the elderly, disabled and increasingly never employed schools leavers.[30]

In 1997 the Scottish Poverty Information Unit identified nine groups of people most vulnerable to poverty: women; unemployed and low paid; lone parents; rural households with low wages and poor access to public services; unemployed 16 and 17 year olds (a category that the Labour Government (1997-) invested heavily in through the *New Deal*); disabled people or families with a disabled child; ethnic minorities; families with children; pensioners.[31] To these we should add one spatial community: areas of urban deprivation (perhaps almost too obvious to have been included) and two further groupings: the homeless and the growing numbers who do not appear on current statistics.

URBAN POVERTY: In the experience of many in the immediate post-war years, the move from the city-centre slums to the newly built peripheral housing schemes was, quite literally, like moving to the Promised Land. But for many the Promised Land has become a desert, largely as a result of poor planning, rapid building and under-investment as well as the advent of mass unemployment. Despite millions of pounds of investment over the last twenty years – much of which made its ways into the pockets and communities of those who worked there but lived somewhere else – there has been little significant improvement in the quality of life for many households. Indeed, for many the situation has only got worse.[32] The Scottish Affairs Committee reported:

> Whilst recognising that there are pockets of poverty throughout Scotland, the impact of poverty is emphasised where whole communities are affected. There are a number of area concentrations in the former industrial communities of west

central Scotland – Inverclyde to Lanarkshire – resulting in general deprivation and health inequalities. Areas in the west fare particularly badly, with about fifty per cent of deprivation areas situated in Glasgow. Significant concentrations can also be found in Edinburgh and Dundee.[33]

It is worth noting that churches, of all denominations, although often very frail, have played an important part in the life of many poor urban communities through the years. Often they have remained committed to an area when others have chosen to leave. James McCormack, Research Director of the Scottish Council Foundation, has noted that churches were among the most trusted organisations in local urban communities.[34] Such compliments, however, should not mask the fact that in all too many cases, the churches have failed poor urban communities, seeking to impose inappropriate models of church life upon them, and then blaming people in those communities for the consequent failure.

RURAL POVERTY: Rural poverty is much harder to define that urban poverty, and the Scottish Executive has commissioned further research to define the level and causes of poverty in rural communities.[35] Nonetheless, it is clear that rural poverty does exist as a significant problem in Scotland with just under 16% of poverty in Scotland in rural communities (46,000 households)[36] The principal causes of rural poverty are broadly similar to urban poverty – unemployment and a low wage economy, elderly households, and changes in the industrial and labour markets[37] – although they are further exacerbated by a higher cost of living, the seasonal nature of employment (e.g. tourism), poor transport infrastructure and a remoteness from services.[38]

WOMEN: It is widely recognised that over the last 20 years there has been a marked increase in the number of women living in poverty, what Pacione refers to as the 'feminisation of poverty.'[39] The UK Human Development Report (2000) records that: 'Overall, women remain one of the largest groups experiencing poverty in the UK. Women constitute 70% of the lowest earners and 56% of the adults living in poverty in the UK. The groups especially at risk from poverty are lone parents and single pensioners.'[40] Women are not only more likely to be living in poverty than men, they are also much more likely to be dealing with its effects as the member of the household most like to have responsibility for managing the family budget.[41]

UNEMPLOYED AND LOW PAID: Training for employment and the creation of employment opportunities has been at the heart of New Labour's social inclusion strategy over the last four years. It clearly sees unemployment as the main cause of poverty in Scotland (and the UK) today.

The Government believes that unemployment is the most important cause of poverty for working age people in Scotland. Its overall anti-poverty strategy is based on tackling what it sees as the causes as well as the symptoms of poverty, by building a welfare system which encourages people into work, helping to develop the skills required by the modern labour market, overcoming labour market problems faced by sections of the working age population and, perhaps most important of all, promoting the full use of potential, especially in childhood. In short, the Government asserts that the key to the strategy lies in tackling the poverty of opportunity[42]

It has increasingly committed itself to a policy of full employment[43] and to making employment worthwhile for those previously dependent upon the benefits systems. At the same time, however, it has introduced fundamental changes to the benefits system – principally through the *Job Seekers Allowance* (JSA) – as a result of which the right to benefit is closely tied to the willingness to accept employment. While there is evidence that the JSA process works well in assisting those in the process from education into work and for those naturally between jobs, it is also increasingly obvious that it is not working in relation to a significant number of young people with deep-rooted problems and temporary or no fixed addresses.[44]

It is difficult to build human and social capital where the conditions that allow people to have self-respect, dignity, security and privacy are absent, and while compulsion measures erode the individual rights of the least advantaged. Further marginalisation occurs in the stigmatisation of unemployed people by repeated reference to fraud and 'dole cheats'; the government's fear of the moral hazard of unemployment seems greater than their concern with the risk to human dignity.[45]

New Labour's employment strategy is heavily dependent upon the presupposition that the UK economy will remain strong and that the jobs being created will be of sufficient quality to lift people out of poverty in the long term. There is evidence that through the 90s many vulnerable young people in particular found themselves caught in a 'black magic roundabout'[46] between unemployment and low paid work. The Minimum Wage and the Working Families Tax Credit have both been introduced to help people to break out of this poverty trap. It is still too soon to be able to analyse the effectiveness of these policies. What is clear, however, is that many commentators believe that these have been set too low. The Church of Scotland's Church and Nation Committee, for example, in evidence given to the Scottish Affairs Committee stated: 'The minimum wage topped up by the working families tax credit and the present levels of income support are below the income levels needed for [the] LCA ('low cost but acceptable') standard of living.'[47] The Scottish Affairs Committee called upon the Government to undertake research to identify a proper level of income adequacy, a task which has not been properly undertaken since 1948.[48]

LONE PARENTS: While lone parent households represent only 5.6% of the population of Scotland, they make up 10.6% of the population who are living in poverty.[49] As we have already noted, many influenced by New Right thinking regard lone parents as part of an *underclass* undermining the nation. In reality, as many with experience would testify, it is remarkable that the vast majority of lone parent households cope as well as they do. Bob Holman, writing of the six people who share their personal stories of poverty in Easterhouse in *Faith in the Poor*, says:

> A Charles Murray snapshot would present Carol as a single mum who gives up the care of her child . . . Anita as the apathetic mother who breeds a heroin addict . . . Erica as a prostitute who bore children by different fathers . . . Denise as the young mum who lounges about indoors . . . Murray would portray them as evidence of the underclass, weak characters whose lack of morals and motivation lead them to poverty and malfunctioning and who are a threat to the nation. But seen from the perspective they present over a long timescale, then they come over as a strong people, who overcome enormous setbacks, who care desperately for their children and who succeed in bringing them up. . . .The deduction is that . . .[they] . . .are not an underclass whose difficulties stem from their wickedness, neglect of children and a rejection of work. Rather, they have to be regarded as people born into many disadvantages and whose efforts to survive are handicapped by conditions of deprivation and poverty. Far from creating poverty, they were flung into it. Given the incomes and surroundings of more affluent citizens, [they] could have contributed much of the distress and want which became the lot of their children.[50]

PEOPLE WITH DISABILITY: Disabled people not only suffer from higher than average levels of poverty – 34% of people with disabilities who are of working age have below half average incomes[51] – but there is also clear evidence that those with disabilities and their carers continue to find themselves excluded from many parts of life in Scotland which others take for granted. 'Modern industrial societies, and even modern welfare states, have been largely constructed on the basis that the people who inhabit them . . .are able-bodied.'[52]

ETHNIC MINORITIES: While there are no official statistics on poverty and ethnicity, it is clear from a range of research that ethnic minorities are much more likely to be living in poverty. According to UK research carried out by Richard Berthoud, 82% of the Pakistani population and 84% of the Bangladeshi population are living at levels of income below half the national average (HBAI).[53] The point is reinforced by the Scottish Poverty Information Unit's 1999 Report which indicates that 'around 60% of Pakistanis and Bangladeshis are poor. This is four times the poverty rate found among white people.'[54] In terms of social exclusion, financial exclusion is merely one component for many from ethnic minorities who, despite over 30 years of race relations legislation, remain disadvantaged in terms of housing, healthcare, social services and education.[55]

CHILDREN: There is a higher rate of child poverty in Britain than in any other country in the EU[56] with over a third of children now living in households experiencing poverty.[57] This represents an over 300% increase on the rates of child poverty in the late 1970s.[58] Although the Scottish Executive has committed itself to the eradication of child poverty within a generation,[59] and the rate according to its own figures has dropped by 4% over the first two years of the New Labour Government (to 30%),[60] it has been criticised for seeking to address child poverty substantially by moving parents back into employment. The Scottish Affairs Committee comments:

> In common with its overall thrust, the Government has based its anti-poverty child strategy on providing opportunities for parents to work. This is all well and good and entirely commendable. . . .On the other hand, some parents might consider that their own nurturing presence was more advantageous to the child. This is a dilemma more common for lone parents.[61]

Cuts in benefits and the connection of *Job Seekers Allowance* to availability for employment has largely removed the option for parents on low income of remaining at home to be with children during pre-school years.

It is estimated that the alleviation of child poverty in Britain would save over 1,400 lives per year.[62] However:

> To alleviate *childhood* poverty requires the alleviation of *family* poverty by raising the living standards and material wealth of all people living in poverty who have children. It also requires raising the living standards of those who do not have children but who are poor – otherwise children continue to be born into poverty. Only a major redistribution of wealth and opportunity coupled with a great increase in the quality of services (especially education) could achieve this.[63]

ELDERLY: While there has been a shift away from the elderly as the primary group affected by poverty over the last 30 years, significant numbers of pensioners continue to live in poverty and the numbers of elderly people living in poverty has continued to rise in real terms. For example, the proportion of single-pensioner households living on or below half the average levels of income (HBAI) has risen from 12% in 1979 to 33% in 1995/6 and for a pensioner couple from 21% to 24%.[64] An often complicated benefits system means that many pensioners do not claim the full level of support to which they are entitled.[65] The most vulnerable groups of pensioners continue to be those who are not entitled to the state pension (around 6%) and those who have not made sufficient National Insurance contributions to entitle them to the full state pension.[66] These are predominantly women. While the level of poverty among people in old age remains intolerably high, it needs to be recognised that in Britain many thousands die each year because of poverty before they reach old age.[67]

HOMELESS: It is estimated that between 8-10,000 Scots per year spend at least one night sleeping rough.[68] However, those sleeping rough, while especially vulnerable, make up a relatively small percentage of Scotland's real homeless figures. In 1982/83 there were 16,523 households in Scotland applying to the local authorities as homeless.[69] By 1997/98 this figures had increased to 43,135.[70] Many homeless people are unable to get employment, or to sustain it if they do. 'The plight of the homeless is a disgrace to modern Scotland.'[71]

THE UNCOUNTED: Many homeless people are not even included in some of the calculations of levels of poverty in Scotland. For example, the *Family Expenditure Survey* (FSE) – an annual government survey of family income and expenditure – excludes people living in institutions such as nursing homes, residential centres, hospitals and prisons, and the homeless.[72] This constitutes between 1.7 and 2.1% of the UK population. According to David Robinson, commenting primarily upon the situation in East London:

> Our experience suggests that this uncounted population is largely made up of refugees, asylum-seekers, travellers and others – mainly 16- to 24-year olds – who are, for whatever reason, transient and 'off register', as well as significant numbers of the very poorest people who disappeared when the Poll Tax was introduced in 1988 [1987 in Scotland]. Almost certainly, some are here illegally or want to preserve their anonymity for particular reasons. Most, however, have nothing to hide and haven't consciously hidden. They are simply outside and unable to find a way in.[73]

There can be no doubt that significant numbers of similar groups exist in Scotland, particularly within our poorest communities. These individuals are not only excluded, but uncounted. As Robinson points out:

> Until we account for the Uncounted, some of our poorest areas will live with a degree of deprivation that most of us would think unthinkable in 21st-century Britain, many will experience community services that are grossly overstretched and thus measurably inferior to comparable services elsewhere and everyone of us will live in a society that has turned down, by default or by design, the willing and vibrant contribution of a significant minority.[74]

The Uncounted and all those living in poverty in Scotland, and beyond, present a challenge to both the Government and the churches.

THE PERFORMANCE OF GOVERNMENT

In many ways it is still too early to determine the success of New Labour's overall anti-poverty strategy. This is, in part, because of the determination of the UK Government, to remain within the spending plans of the previous administration when it came to power in 1997. As a result, key elements of its strategy – such as the minimum wage, the working families tax credit and minimum income guarantee for pensioners – are only at this stage being implemented. This, combined with the inevitable delay between implementation and evidence of impact, and the recognised inadequacy of effective data in many areas, means that any evaluation remains incomplete.

The vision of the Scottish Executive was spelt out in its 1999 *Social Justice Report*. It stated its desire for:

◆ A Scotland in which every child matters, where every child, regardless of their family background, has the best possible start in life.
◆ A Scotland in which every young person has the opportunities, skills and support to make a successful transition to working life and active citizenship.
◆ A Scotland in which every family is able to support itself – with work for those who can and security for those who can't.
◆ A Scotland in which every person beyond working age has a decent quality of life.
◆ A Scotland in which every person both contributes to and benefits from the community in which they live.[75]

In outlining this vision, the Scottish Executive set a series of targets which included 'ending child poverty within a generation, full employment by providing opportunities for all those who can work, and securing dignity for older people.'[76] Commendably it has published 29 milestones against which it wishes its performance to be tracked. In its September 2000 budget it committed itself to a major injection into public sector finance. According to the Executive:

An extra £6 billion is being injected into Scottish services over the next three years, targeted to help tackle inequalities. Health spending will increase by nearly 15%; Education by nearly 17% and the Social Justice and Housing budget goes up by 20% after allowing for inflation . . .

Across the Executive, a wide-ranging set of policies have been put in place to address social exclusion. Over time, and in conjunction with the measures being put in place by the UK Government, they amount to the most serious attack on poverty and inequality for generations.[77]

While this may well be true, the previous 20 years have been marked by a massive increase in levels of poverty in the UK and the reversal of centuries of growing equality between the richest and poorest.

To tackle the now deep-rooted nature of poverty and inequality will require more radical measures than have been widely in evidence to date. At the root of these must lie a real commitment to redistribution of wealth. While there has been a welcome investment in the public sector – funded in large measure through the successful economy – to support the poorest in our society, our tax system continues to favour the rich.

Since 1980, government policies on taxation have favoured the better off, with the top rate of tax being reduced from 84 to 40%. . . .There also has been a shift from tax on income (direct taxation) to tax on expenditure (indirect taxation) . . .which has a disproportionate effect on the poorest groups. The overall effect has been to move the burden of tax from the rich to the poor, so that by 1995 'the poorest fifth paid more of their income in tax – 27% in 1983 versus 39% in 1995 – than the richest fifth – 41% in 1985 versus 36% in 1995.'[78]

New Labour has done little to alter this reality. Although it makes uncomfortable reading for many, the reality is that poverty is not the fault of the *underclass*, nor even the inevitable consequence of globalisation and changes in the world economy. Poverty in Britain is largely caused by the non-poor and by the unwillingness of the Government to ask them to play their part in the creation of a fairer society. According to David Byrne:

> 'Exclusion' is something that is done by some people to other people. The central tenet of the popular version of 'the underclass' argument is that miserable conditions are self-induced – the poor do it to themselves. Political theorists of social exclusion allow that they can be consequences of economic transformation; it is the fault of 'society' as a whole. So far only dangerous radicals, like the Catholic Bishops of England and Wales, admit that the people who stand to gain might have something to do with it – that they might be shaping the character of economic and social arrangements, the very stuff of social politics, to their own advantage and to the disadvantage of others.[79]

At some point, if poverty and inequality are going to be effectively challenged in our society, the Government will require to have the moral courage to place a greater tax burden upon the rich.

Any programme to lower inequality must surely address the incomes and privileges of the rich. The marginal rates of both income tax and inheritance tax should be higher; everybody knows it, especially the rich. Property taxes are too low, and there should be a higher rate of tax for luxuries, so that higher value goods bought by the rich people provide proportionally more tax. The upper earnings limit for National Insurance contributions should also be removed. At least £5 billion of extra cash could be paid each year by the rich.[80]

The New Labour Government has been right to identify unemployment as the major cause of poverty in Britain today, but it has been wrong to focus upon employment creation as the principal method of overcoming poverty for many. While it has been relatively successful in the delivery of the first half of its celebrated mantra – 'work for those who can' – it has still to show evidence of its commitment to the second half – 'security for those who cannot.' Income Support is now down to around 20% of average earnings.[81] The Scottish Affairs Committee noted the evidence of the Zacchaeus 2000 Trust that the last time benefits rates were set at a standard by what they could actually buy was in 1948, and the Committee recommended the introduction of a properly researched 'minimum incomes yardstick which is sensitive to local conditions.'[82] Such a figure needs to become the yardstick against which benefit levels are measured.

The Scottish Affairs Committee also called for a review of the working of the Social Fund.[83] In 1994 the Commission on Social Justice, set up by the then Labour leader John Smith, stated that 'perhaps the most soul-destroying aspect of Income Support is the Social Fund.'[84] In recent years the churches have joined with others through the *Debt on our Doorstep* campaign to call upon the Government to change a system which is failing the poor. In 1999/2000, 362,000 applications for a loan were refused on the basis that the applicants would be unable to repay any loan which was made![85]

The people who are the real experts on poverty are the poor. The Government, and perhaps more so, the Scottish Executive, have begun to make limited efforts to incorporate poor people in policy making and practice.[86] However, as Bob Holman points out: 'The heralded involvement of those in "socially excluded" communities has yet to materialise. The Social Exclusion Unit has "excluded the excluded".'[87] Holman's suggestions of a National Neighbourhood Fund controlled by local neighbourhood groups in deprived areas rather than the existing framework in which local community representatives often feel largely excluded from the decision-making process needs to be taken very seriously. Above all the voice of poor people requires to be heard and acted upon. Jane Tewson, the founder of Charity Projects and co-founder of Comic Relief has written: 'The truth is that it's people who have been through the mill themselves who often have the most to contribute, and the best ideas for workable solutions.'[88]

AND FOR THE CHURCH?

While the Government can claim a responsibility to govern 'on behalf of all the people,' the Church has a calling to identify with Jesus who is to be found among the poorest and the least.[89] Although there are many reports from the various churches in Scotland calling upon the UK Government and Scottish Executive to give priority to the needs of the poorest, there are relatively few examples of such practice in the life of the Church. It is often the churches in the poorest areas of Scotland – rural and urban – which are closed (or rationalised) while congregations in wealthy communities continue because they have the local resources. The Joseph Rowntree Foundation in evidence to the Scottish Affairs Committee suggested that 'far from engaging and assisting disadvantaged communities, the private sector was in fact withdrawing from these areas.'[90] The same could be said of the churches. If the Gospel is to be enacted as 'good news to the poor'[91] then this will have to change. Elaine Graham is right: 'the reality of the Gospel is primarily manifested in living communities of justice and hope and only derivatively in prepositional truth-claims.'[92] Words are not enough. The more progressive tax system which has been advocated by the Church for the Government to adopt needs also to be put into place within the churches. This, combined with a greater practical willingness for the different denominations within a community to work together to make a difference, could begin to make a significant difference in poor communities.

This is not to suggest that the churches in Scotland are doing nothing to assist people living in poverty. There is a considerable amount of valuable and important work going on, organised at both a national level through the various social care branches of the churches and at a local, congregational level. The work of the Scottish Churches Community Trust supporting church based community work on an ecumenical basis is an important symbol of what is possible. However, such work remains largely at the fringes of the churches and is primarily about delivering services for poor people rather than struggling alongside the poor for justice.

If our answer is to be with the poor, then what is the most appropriate model for mission? Historically, the church has primarily sought to serve the poor. Charity and support for various health, education and other development projects have been the main response. However, this model has chiefly focused on the symptoms of poverty without addressing the root causes behind it. Therefore, to address the foundations on which poverty is based, to confront the sources of poverty, will require a reorientation of the way in which we have engaged in mission in the past; it will require us to place advocacy and solidarity at the centre of the church's mission programmes. This is not a new strategy as advocacy and solidarity have been a longstanding part of mission; but like the marginalised for whom it seeks to be an advocate, it has been on the margins of our mission agendas.[93]

Churches which are serious about enabling people to break out of poverty will have to learn to walk alongside poor people, and be instructed by them. This will be a hard and costly road for many. Its route was in some way laid out in a British Council of Churches book of the late 1980s.

In Britain we are called to a theology of solidarity. . . .We must begin to see this as the new ecumenical adventure in which we must engage. The only reconciliation possible to us is through solidarity with the poor. This unity we seek with the poor has to be deep and committed. This means following their lead and direction, not on whim or fancy, but on orders. It means bearing burdens and sharing defeat. It is also being prepared to do battle, to demonstrate, to say the unpopular and the uncomfortable. Above all, it is a process of engagement, which step by step converts us as a church, opens our eyes and set us on the way of the Cross.[94]

On the vast majority of occasions when the churches pray for the poor, the poor are referred to as 'them'. The fundamental challenge which faces the Church if it is serious about helping people to break out of poverty, is to develop models, structures and ways of living so as the poor are referred to as 'us'. At that point, while the poor may still be with us, the Church will have begun to succeed in the breaking out of her own poverty of spirit.

CHAPTER TWO

BREAKING INTO A NEW ENLIGHTENMENT

Part I

Spiritual Values and the Knowledge Economy

Gordon Graham

What place, if any, do spiritual values have in the knowledge economy? I raise this question in this form because, as it seems to me, there are two striking facts about contemporary higher education in Scotland that are rarely, if ever, considered together. The first is that those who are now its political masters expect the universities of Scotland to be major contributors to something called 'the knowledge economy'. It is in the light of this expectation that the Scottish Executive structures its decisions about financial support through the agency of the Scottish Higher Education Funding Council. My second observation, and on the surface at any rate, one wholly unconnected with the first, is the fact that amongst our universities, the oldest, and some of the most prestigious still, are religious foundations. This is a matter of recorded history and is thus no less a reality than contemporary educational policy. Can the two be connected in any way? Does religious foundation have anything to do with modern relevance and social importance? Or is it to be forgotten and ignored?

THE ANCIENT UNIVERSITIES OF SCOTLAND

Let me expand upon the second of these facts. Scotland's universities include four of the oldest in Europe. Moreover, they remain among its most distinguished. Unquestionably, the newer institutions have many strengths and virtues, but no one could deny, I think, that the University of Edinburgh is an institution of international standing. So too, in their different ways, are Glasgow, St Andrews and Aberdeen. The last is the resulting combination of two institutions – King's College and

Marischal College – that went their largely separate ways for 250 years until their unification in 1860. All five, however, were religious foundations. It is true that Edinburgh was a civic rather than an ecclesiastical foundation, but its inspiration – Presbyterianism – was no less Christian (and hence no less religious) than the Pre-Reformation foundations at St Andrews, Glasgow and King's (to put them in chronological order). Does this mean anything in the context of modern Scotland? Does ancient foundation have anything to do with contemporary relevance? This is the unfashionable issue I mean to address.

Something of the spirit of all these old foundations is to be discovered in the Papal Bull that established King's College in Old Aberdeen in 1495. In rather splendid wording it says this:

> Now, a petition lately presented to us on the part of our dearest son in Christ, James, illustrious king of Scots, desiring that the condition of his people be improved, and considering that in the north-eastern parts of the said kingdom there are some places, separated from the rest of his kingdom by arms of the sea and very high mountains, in which dwell men who are rude, ignorant of letters and almost barbarous and who, on account of the over great distance from the places in which universities flourish and the dangerous passage to such places, cannot have leisure for the study of letters, nay, are so ignorant of these letters that suitable men cannot be found not only for the preaching of the Word of God to the people of those places, but even for the administering of the sacraments; and that if in the famous city of Old Aberdeen, which is near enough to the places foresaid, there should flourish a university in every lawful faculty, very many men of the said kingdom, and especially those parts, would apply themselves to such study of letters and acquire that most precious pearl of knowledge, the ignorant would be informed, and the rude become learned.

The words, we may reasonably suppose, reflect the views and aspirations of its founder Bishop William Elphinstone. Elphinstone was a man of remarkable vision. His natural context was that of Europe; he himself studied law at Paris. He was also a diplomat of some consequence, and familiar with the intricacies of international negotiation. Yet his principal and most enduring aspiration was for the locality of the North East, and his ambition for it was to secure the foundation of a university both like and equal to that of his world writ large. In short, his aim was to counter parochialism.

The means by which he sought to do so – university education – repay examination. First it is to be observed that he put the Christian religion at the heart of it, literally. Geographically, the famous King's College Chapel, with its distinctive mediaeval crown tower, which almost uniquely remains unaltered since its foundation stone was laid in 1500, is at the centre of the modern university. I will return to the question of its contemporary position, intellectually speaking. Second, contrary to the contentions of some modern-day purists who deplore, as they see it, the incursion of practical training into the curricula of universities, his purpose was in considerable part education for the professions. Indeed it is a notable fact that King's College was (possibly) the first European university to include a Mediciner amongst its Foundation Chairs. This fact can be blown up to indefensible significance; it is to be doubted whether effective medical education played much of a part in the first few centuries of the new university at Aberdeen. Nonetheless, the establishment of this Chair at the outset is an important indicator of Elphinstone's intent – that the education his university offered would be practical as well as edifying.

I cite these facts not in order to eulogise the past (though I think there is indeed something admirable to contemplate in it) but in order to point to a feature of the four ancient universities of Scotland (not just Aberdeen) that I believe to be of some significance. That is to say, they sought, from the early period of their existence, to combine the liberal arts with training for the professions. The structure within which they sought to do so is reasonably well known. All students entered the 'lower' Faculty of Arts, where they studied some variation on the traditional mediaeval curriculum of the seven liberal arts, and only then could they proceed to the 'higher' Faculties of Divinity, Law and Medicine, which only a small proportion did as a matter of fact. Surprisingly, perhaps, it was a structure that, with many imperfections, survived over several centuries, longer in Scotland than any other European country indeed.

But that was long ago. A series of Government prompted reforms in the course of the nineteenth century led to an altered, though settled pattern of university education that preserved something of the Scottish tradition for about seventy years. Then the vastly increased dependence of the universities on state funding together with the influence of educational fashions combined to end, more or less, a centuries old tradition that lent distinctiveness to Scottish higher education. Today, despite occasional public protestations to the contrary, the Scottish universities are not notably different from their other British counterparts, and imitate, if they do not exactly realize, features of similar institutions in Europe and North America.

The early twentieth century picture changed still further, thanks to the gradual assimilation of mechanics institutes and colleges of technology into the university system. In 1900 there were four universities in Scotland, all with a long history. By the year 2000 there were fourteen, many of which were relatively recent creations and all with widely differing origins. It is to this system that the Scottish Parliament and Scottish Executive looks to provide a large part of the basis of the 'knowledge economy', and thus perform the function that contemporary society is believed to require of them. Do the purposes of the ancient foundations have anything to say in this context?

Lest I be thought to be engaging in romanticism, and lamenting, in a nostalgic vein, the loss of the past, let me say at once that I do not believe in any concept of 'the good old days'. Just as there are no 'brave new worlds' so there were no 'good old days'. This does not mean, however, that the past has nothing to teach us about the present, and in order to explore the lessons that it might have for us, I want to look more closely at the dominant conception at work in contemporary policy with respect to universities – the idea of 'the knowledge economy'.

PROSPERITY VERSUS ENRICHMENT

What is a 'knowledge economy' exactly? I cannot say that I have come across any clear account of its meaning; public pronouncements on the issue are generally clouded in jargon. At the same time, it is not hard to guess what people who are willing to use the phrase have in mind. There is a widespread belief that the state of the modern world is one in which familiarity with innovative technologies is essential to economic prosperity. 'Fitting the nation for the 21st century' is another commonly used expression that encapsulates the same idea. Now this much is true; many jobs require a knowledge of the new media – such things as computers, the Internet, e-mail and electronic marketing techniques. There is also bio-technology. Food processing and supply, the development of medications and the production of new materials are clearly a feature of the world in which we live that cannot be ignored. At the same time, there has been a recorded shift from manufacturing to service industries. The finance sector, insurance, and government bureaucracy for that matter, are major employers. Perhaps it is true that it is not possible to hold down a job in one of these areas without being computer literate and familiar with all the apparatus of electronic communication. I say 'perhaps' because it seems to me equally obvious that much of the service sector – the supermarkets, pub chains and leisure complexes that have made such a prominent appearance in contemporary life – requires of most of those employed in them a relatively elementary knowledge of these new technologies. They need to operate the machines, certainly, but they need know virtually nothing of the technology that went into their manufacture.

Two important facts have brought about this situation. First, the whole tendency in modern technology, especially information technology, has been in the direction of 'user friendliness'. That is to say, it has proved in the interests of manufacturers to make information technology require *less* knowledge of the science that underlies it rather than more. When I first took up computer technology the amount of special instruction I required was quite high. But now there is far greater appeal to the intuitive; what seems obvious and natural turns out to be what works. Apple computers set the standard in this regard, and PCs have followed. The development of both has meant that the use of computers requires very little special training. Institutions run special courses, but there is a genuine question in many instances as to how far these are truly needed. There is certainly specialist software in which people require training, but the profitability of selling huge numbers of computers to ordinary people has been a powerful commercial impetus to ensure that there is a great deal of software for which this is not the case.

For instance, most modern tills work not on codes that must be learned, but on pictures and icons whose meaning is evident, and the average checkout operator requires nothing more than the ability to pass a barcode in front of a reading device. Likewise, the technology of the ATM – the cash machine – which almost everyone has rapidly managed to master, requires no special training. This is an example worth dwelling on. Could anyone seriously suggest that the operation of these machines, which have played such a large part in the expansion of contemporary commerce, requires university educated operators? I take this to be a rhetorical question. The truth, on the contrary, is that quite deliberately ATMs have been made accessible to and operable by the least technologically minded In the light of this example, it is easy to see that only a blind adherence to the dogma of 'the knowledge economy' could incline anyone to think that the success of major technological advances requires special educational provision.

Second, there is this important fact – the operation of many pieces of hi-tech machinery is readily mastered by children without lessons being devoted to it. It is standardly remarked that often it is the pupils rather than the teacher who have first, and more easily, mastered the technology of the video-recorder and the computer. What does this imply? It implies that any formal effort put into technical training may well be a waste of time and resources, that children, left to their own devices, can learn these things rapidly and easily. They do so because they quickly see the advantages of doing so. As a result they want to master them. If this is true then at least at this level, 'the knowledge economy' can take care of itself, and needs no state funded provision.

Where then does the need for *special* provision lie? The answer that is often given has to do with flexibility. According to this common contention, whereas formerly people were trained in a specific skill that they and their employers expected to last them a lifetime, nowadays we need to educate people in a way that will enable them to adapt to whatever the fast moving times in which we live may throw up next, though whether this sharp contrast between past and present is really justifiable seems to me questionable. However, if what I have been saying is correct, such adaptability will not need much special training, and will be something to which people accommodate themselves prettily readily. Machinery, there is every reason to think, will become even more user friendly, and natural curiosity, assisted by practical benefit, will lead most people to master it.

Even where there is need for special training, this may not imply much about the curricula of schools and universities. Arguably, no technological development has ever had so great an impact on the way human beings live than the motor car. For most people today, the ability to drive a car is essential. Yet driving, which *does* need special lessons, has played no part in the formal curriculum of our educational institutions. It has not needed to. The evident desirability of being able to drive, and the general desire to do so, have been stimuli enough to make it happen. And, it might be added, neither the requirement to pay for such instruction nor the introduction of government oversight of its provision and assessment, has pushed it into those institutions. Debates about educational policy and provision and arguments over the introduction of fees would benefit greatly, in my view, from closer attention to this humble but hugely important form of mass education.

These remarks imply, what I in fact believe, that there is an absurd overestimation, a mythology in fact, about the novelty of modern technology and about the need for our educational system to address it.

I do not think that it has been shown, or even made plausible, that formal education in new technologies is a *sine qua non* of employment in a modern economy, and in so far as money is poured into state institutions with this as their purpose, it is money wasted. But what interests me much more than this is an unspoken but important assumption that lies behind all this talk of 'the knowledge economy'. This assumption may be broadly described as utilitarian, and it is one of very great significance. It is the assumption that university education (to which I am confining myself here) is to be valued chiefly for its contribution to economic prosperity.

In order to challenge this assumption effectively it is necessary to issue some disclaimers. I have no wish to deny that economic prosperity is important. It is fashionable in some quarters – not very many it is true – to decry materialism, and to assume at the same time that objections to materialism are objections to the pursuit of economic advancement. This seems to me importantly false. Wealth creation is something that almost everyone who has not been indoctrinated in a certain sort of socialism welcomes. At the same time, no one need hold, nor ought they to hold, that economic advancement, in the sense of increased purchasing power, is in itself a significant form of enrichment. To put the point at its simplest: those who have a lot of money are no better off if they have nothing to spend it on. More importantly yet, they are no better off if they have nothing *better* to spend it on. This further thought is, interestingly, underlined by an economic principle – the principle of diminishing marginal utility. This states that we are increasingly less well-off, strange as this may sound, the more of a good we have. For example, to own a car for the first time is a real benefit. But if I already have a car, a second car is of much less benefit. There are relatively fewer things that I can now do that I could not do before. When it comes to a fifth or sixth car, there is almost no increase in benefit. Similarly, to be able for the first time to afford to eat out once a week is a real improvement in my general welfare. But to have money enough to eat out, say, fifty times a week, is not fifty times the benefit of the first. There is a limit to how many restaurant meals I can savour, let alone eat.

To make my point most plainly I need to introduce some stipulative terminology. I want to contrast wealth with enrichment. In so far as wealth means simply increased purchasing power it does not of itself imply enrichment, except in the restricted and uninteresting sense of more money. If advantage in 'the knowledge economy' is confined to increased earning opportunities, therefore, it is erroneously thought of as a species of enrichment. This is as true of societies as of individuals, a point to which I shall return. To be enriched, in this sense, we need an increase in value and not merely in wealth. The important question for present purposes is how that value is to be increased if not by mere earning capacity. The answer it seems to me is plain; we need to create more things worth spending money on. Now what are these to be?

It is evident to my mind, that enrichment properly so called is not an increase in purchasing power but the creation of new benefits, new 'goods' if you like. Some of these, of course, will be material goods – a better range and quality of foods, new and better forms of entertainment, travel and medical provision. But it is worth noting that these examples, which contemporary opinion readily endorses, are limited in important ways. The first two have to do with pleasure, essentially. Good food (leaving aside its nutritional properties) and good entertainment realize the underlying value of pleasure. *Pace* a certain sort of Puritanism this is indeed a value, but it is not the only one. Improved medical provision relates to health, a value that is to be distinguished from pleasure. Health, it is important to observe, increases both the vitality and the length of life of the individual. In itself, though, it is curiously empty. What is that increased vitality and longevity to be spent doing? A long and healthy life spent in isolation and boredom, or worse degradation and humiliation, is a curse, not a benefit. It is precisely this sort of condition in which people are driven to the thought 'I wish I had never been born'. Better health in other words, is a neutral improvement in the human condition. Its value depends on other improvements. Of course, the other benefit I noted that 'the knowledge economy' promises us – pleasure – provides part of an answer. Our increased vitality and longevity, if good food and good entertainment are what are on offer, are to be occupied with pleasurable activities. Here however, there looms a daunting, and in the literal sense I think, dispiriting prospect – that the ultimate purpose presenting itself is that of 'amusing ourselves to death' (as Neil Postman has it).

CULTURAL ENRICHMENT AND THE OLD UNIVERSITIES

What might the alternatives be? The answer is not so very far to seek. As well as enjoyment, a healthy and a long life is enriched by opportunities for intellectual engagement, aesthetic enlargement, public participation and moral endeavour, to name only some of the alternatives to 'amusing ourselves to death'. But what supplies such opportunities? The answer is at least threefold; it is the existence of longstanding traditions, well established practices and social institution. Amongst the traditions are such things as historical consciousness (a part of which is what people call 'national identity'), a shared sense of the value of learning and the exercise of civic responsibility. Among the practices are science, literature, law, music and the other arts, parliamentary democracy, agriculture and industry. Among the institutions are museums, art galleries, churches, hospitals, orchestras, the courts, the press, schools, radio and television, trade associations, libraries and most significant for my purposes, universities.

The ancient universities of Scotland were to this degree special; they made it part of their purpose to promote reflective engagement with the culture, religion and professions of the society in which they were situated. In this there is something of a contrast to be drawn with the ancient universities of England – Oxford and Cambridge. In England there was not the structure of lower and higher faculties, and professional education was in large part provided elsewhere – in the Inns of Court and the Colleges of Physicians and Surgeons. In the eighteenth century the University of Edinburgh led the world in the study of anatomy, while Oxford languished in anything that might be called a scientific education. The Professors of Moral Philosophy, Adam Smith at Glasgow and Adam Ferguson at Edinburgh, especially the former, were founding figures in the study of economy and society. There was no counterpart in England. The great political philosophers John Locke and Thomas Hobbes never held university appointments. In Scotland graduates from the lower Faculty of Arts supplied schools with teachers while in England 'ushers' arose from within the school system itself.

The contrast should not be overdrawn, however. Indeed, far from wishing to stress the superiority of Scottish universities, my purpose is better served by drawing attention to the multifarious ways in which all the universities of Britain, and of Europe, contributed to the emergence of cultural, social and political organizations of great importance. For instance, though the British Museum, which advertises itself as the oldest in the world, was created by Act of Parliament, Oxford University's Ashmolean Museum pre-dates it by some seventy years. Who could doubt that the museum, a most wonderful combination of science and history, has hugely contributed to the traditions of both? Similarly, it was the academic presses of Oxford and Cambridge, which had no significant counterparts in Scotland, that made the technology of the book into the great organ of the diffusion of letters that it has become. Let it be said, too, the universities cannot claim a monopoly on cultural accretion. It is to State and aristocratic patronage that we must credit most of the visual art that we now enjoy. Similarly, it was the

Church and court, not universities, that supplied the greatest stimulus to music. Indeed, it is recordable that the study of music within the seven liberal arts of the mediaeval university did relatively little to stimulate music making and composition. These finally found a world of their own for the most part outside the universities.

Nonetheless, though the true story is complex, it is unquestionably the case that universities across Europe, and later in the United States of America, were crucial in sustaining, reflecting upon and advancing the traditions, practices and institutions that go to make up the sources of our enrichment. Historical study does not merely stock the museums; it interprets the meaning of their stock, in much the same way that the study of art is related to its creation. Science and medical faculties do not merely advance science and medicine; they also take stock of those advances. Law Faculties seek to relate the work of the Courts to wider conceptions of justice. In short, when they are working well and in accordance with their proper purpose, universities are places that enrich the society to which they belong. But if so, the principal form of the enrichment we can look to universities to provide is *not* the generation of increased earning power. Rather they stimulate, assimilate and assess the goods upon which any increase in our earnings is to be spent.

The mistake of thinking otherwise is twofold; it supposes falsely that universities are specially good places in which to learn how to increase earning potential. Some may be. It is unquestionably true that there are aspects of university research and education, especially in the newer universities, that are directly connected with increased economic prosperity. I have no desire to deny this, and indeed welcome it. What I seek to deny, however, is that this is the chief claim that universities have upon public approval and support. If it were, a great deal of what goes on in some of its best and most prestigious departments would have nothing to commend it. To take only my own subject: Scottish philosophy, somewhat surprisingly for such a small nation, can more than hold its own in the full sweep of intellectual history – David Hume, Thomas Reid and Adam Smith have relatively few rivals in the intellectual firmament. However, they make a poor showing in the narrowly economic stakes if we take Henry Ford, Richard Branson or Bill Gates as our standard.

In the second place, at the risk of attracting the opprobrium of many of my colleagues in the universities, who are stuggling hard to persuade the Government that they have a legitimate claim upon the public purse, I am inclined to think that, despite all the talk of transferable skills, students who master the challenging subjects of genetics, metaphysics,

Hebrew, plate tectonics or pure mathematics, are not notably better at enterprise and innovation. While it may be in the interests of university managers at the present time to claim that university education equips the nation with its entrepreneurial talent – a claim much in accord with public policy of course – my own belief is that it simply is not so. The error in thinking that the value of higher education in itself (there are obvious exceptions) lies in its contribution to earning potential is disguised by the fact that talented people are indeed likely to succeed in *both* universities *and* in business. Real talent is relatively rarely confined to just one type of activity. But to pretend that its success in business is *a result of* its success in universities is, in my view, to connive at a deception.

If this is so, if university study is in large part *useless*, what then is to be said for universities? In answer to this question I want to emphasis once more that earning potential cannot plausibly be construed as the ultimate source of enrichment. To be wealthier is not in and of itself to be richer; I am no better off, however great my income, if I have nothing better to buy.

To pursue this issue further there is point in returning to the original foundation of our most venerable institutions and to the topic of spiritual values. Let us suppose, contrary to some of the things I have been saying, that 'the knowledge economy' is an essential precondition of prosperity in the century that is beginning. If I am right, there is still this question: What is the increased income the knowledge economy generates to be spent on? It could of course be spent on mere gratification – more computer games, more gossip magazines, more videos and television quiz programmes. But is there nothing more significant that we might purchase with it? The answer is that there is, *if* there are healthy traditions, practices and institutions in place to supply it.

If there are, or more accurately, if there are to be, they will be institutions that aspire to the edification and the enlargement of human horizons, that will reflectively sustain all those things I enumerated earlier – a sense of identity, civic responsibility, science, law, the arts and political participation. In short, we need institutions that hold out ambitions greater than those of immediate gratification and passing entertainment. Where are such institutions to be found? I do not know that they are to be found anywhere, if they are not to be found in our universities. Universities are not unique in this, let me repeat, but they play an important part, and moreover a role much in keeping with the Scottish tradition.

Suppose it is so, suppose that the peculiar role of the university is not that of increasing income generation so much as supplying and sustaining the ultimate goods on which increased income is to be spent. Does this invoke the idea of *spiritual* values, the subject we began with? The rejection of the supernatural is almost a defining characteristic of our culture. This does not necessarily imply a negative answer because there is a use, and a meaning, of the expression 'the spiritual' that does not point to some transcendent realm, but confines it to the world we know. Consider the familiar phrase 'triumph of the human spirit'. The human spirit, as the modern world speaks of it, is to be encountered in many of the things I have alluded to – scientific theorizing, musical composition, artistic vision, political leadership, the pursuit of justice. If we focus upon the human spirit and invoke no other spirits, divine or angelic, we seem to have a spiritual counter to the materialistic inclinations of our time without any super-naturalistic overtones. If this is so, then we need only return to the founding principles of our ancient universities in part; .something like the non-utilitarian explanation of the value of universities and other cultural institutions can be defended with a conception of spiritual value that requires no appeal to Christian or other religious values.

MEANING AND MATERIALISM

I believe this to be one of the greatest challenges that contemporary Christianity faces — not the onslaught of materialism – which I think the argument I have presented shows to be relatively easy to refute – but an alternative account of spiritual values, the triumph of a new humanism over an outmoded religion. What, if anything, does the Christian have to say in reply? And how does it relate to universities?

The answer, if there is one, begins with this thought: humanism depends upon the Protagorean doctrine that 'man is the measure of all things'. The normal expansion of this familiar saying (not an historically accurate one, it may be) runs: 'of that which is, that it is, and of that which is not, that it is not'. Protagoras was an ancient Greek philosopher, but the doctrine with which his name is associated is fashionable again in the realms of postmodernism. But can we really believe this? Could it be true that it is human beings that are the measure of what exists and what does not? Interestingly it is religion's most widely perceived opponent – natural science – that gives us most reason to doubt Protagoras's claim and natural science is the sphere in which postmodernism has made least impact. This is because

Protagorean relativism flies in the face of the spectacular, and progressive, advances that have been made in physics, chemistry and biology. However plausible the allegations of the protagoreans and postmodernists may be with respect to the humanities and social sciences, they lose all their plausibility when it comes these.

Not many people will deny this, I expect, but I want to point to an implication it has that is specially relevant here. Suppose it is true that the worlds studied by physics and biology exist independently of the human mind, there is still this question: what is the point and the value of studying them? If the answer to *this* question is a matter entirely relative to human purposes and values, what is it? If the *value* of science is to be explained in terms other than its usefulness, and if the world of values is nonetheless bounded by the interests of humans, then the only explanation we can give for the value of pure science lies in human curiosity and its desire to know.

Now about this we might make the following observation. Human curiosity is a very varied thing. Human beings can be curious about the most trivial affairs. If human interest is the ultimate explanation of the value of science, it is a very poor one. Gossip magazines satisfy human curiosity at least as well, if not better, than anything universities have to offer. In short, the satisfaction of human curiosity is a value indifferent to the huge gap between gossip and science, and trivializes the magisterial understanding that the latter has to offer.

There is much more to be said, but here I will rest content with asserting that the real explanation of the value of science, and of all non-utilitarian branches of learning must lie elsewhere, in something rather larger and of greater import than the human spirit humanly conceived.

It is at this point that we have reason to return to the aspirations of Bishop Elphinstone, exemplified by the chapel he put at the heart of his university. The truth, as he saw it, is that in the life of the mind and the explorations of the intellect, we reach beyond the human and begin to see and to appreciate, albeit dimly, the mind that *made* the world in which we have our three score years and ten, a world which we certainly cannot fashion but which, mysteriously, we can hope to understand. To provide a full scale modern defence of this conception would be a major undertaking, something I have only gestured at here. But it seems to me true that, in the conspicuous absence of any other answer, by regarding their religious foundation as irrelevant and their chapels as marginal, the ancient universities of Scotland run the risk of eliminating their own purposes, and emptying their most fundamental activities of meaning.

Part II

Education and Vision

Elizabeth Templeton

CURRENT BARBARISM AND THE NEED FOR ENLIGHTENMENT

I remember coming home to Britain in 1987 after six months living abroad. Thatcherism was penetrating every institution in the land. In the first television news broadcast I watched, an eminent brain surgeon was being interviewed about pioneering new techniques he had evolved for brain surgery in very young babies. 'These operations,' observed the interviewer, 'are fiendishly expensive. Given all the pressures on the NHS, can we really justify spending so much on this one area of specialised work?'

'But you must remember,' the surgeon retorted, 'if these children recover, they will be viable economic units.'

A nation which needs such a justification for curing sick children has reverted to a new barbarism. But the insidious spread of a culture which values everything in terms of market efficiency has been so steady that even a Labour politician in the Scottish Parliament could, a few months ago, suggest that the underlying goal of the educational enterprise at the school level was 'to equip children for the global market'.

The prioritising within the National Curriculum south of the border of literacy, numeracy and I.T. has had little difficulty in migrating northwards, as the Scottish Executive's document 'Improving Our Schools' made clear. Subjects like Art, Music, Drama, History are being squeezed from the curriculum under the intense pressure to improve competence in the more marketable skills of the dominant core subjects. Nurseries are being directed to earlier and earlier introduction of these elements of the formal curriculum. Teacher training is increasingly dispensing with the history, philosophy or sociology of education, and concentrating on issues of delivery, progression and assessment within the classroom. And once inside that classroom, teachers are faced with such an array of named targets to be achieved in finite time that there is little opportunity for reflection on the purposes and values of the educational process.

When I began my work with the Christian Education Movement in

1995, providing support in the field of Religious and Moral Education, I had the privilege of visiting many schools to discover what happened in the R.E. classroom, or in primary schools, in that curriculum slot. Over and over again, particularly in primary schools, teachers reported that the area they found hardest to handle in the curriculum guidelines was that headed 'Personal Search: ultimate questions'. And when asked to explain why, the answer was, with depressing frequency: 'because we don't know the answers'. The idea that it might be one role of a teacher to share the exploring of unanswerable questions was, apparently, unthought, if not unthinkable.

MYTH AND REALITY IN THE SCOTTISH ENLIGHTENMENT

I do not want to contrast this general state of affairs with some myth of Scottish Enlightenment which generates false nostalgia, or idealises the past. To have the elite of the land reading Cicero at six while the peasants and urban poor went about their God-appointed tasks on land and in factory was no Utopia. It was not, after all, until 1872 that compulsory primary education was centrally organised and inspected, in spite of the Reformation vision of 'a school in every parish': and the support of basic Bible reading literacy for all.

As late as 1950, when I entered primary school, the classroom was still organised so that the illiterate and woefully underprivileged children, who came to school without proper coats or shoes or breakfasts, sat in a state of permanent degradation at the front of the class, wiping their noses on their sleeves, and being belted many times a week.

I share with Professor Graham, however, a conviction that the so-called 'Age of Enlightenment' was more than a fashionable and self-congratulatory construct by a clique of Europe's meritocrats. The political revulsion of the early 18th century at the earlier wars of religion: the gradual extension of the franchise: the repeal of oppressive legislation: the human rights movements which campaigned against slavery and child labour: the development of international law – all of these emerged from a passion of the heart, not just from a narrow rationalism. Certainly, as we look back, we can see that the Enlightenment cosmos was too tidy, too confident of the inevitability of progress, too certain that human reason could explain and measure everything, too unaware of its own shadow side. Yet, for all its limitations, the valuing of education as a tool for growth and social participation was a genuine movement of the spirit, concern to nurture what Professor George Davie has written of as 'The Democratic Intellect'.[1]

That a person is much more than an intellect need not, I suppose, be argued in this company; but that there are *real* connections between the development of intellectual skills and human well-being, the ability to understand and question and criticise the status quo, let alone the more obvious gains in say medicine or nutrition, should not be forgotten.

It is not, however, the primary concern of my 'subtext' to evaluate the 18th century Enlightenment, which is now widely deconstructed as an imbalanced and arrogantly complacent phase of European and Scottish culture. What I am concerned to do is to sketch what it might mean to break into a *new* enlightenment, one which might reflect the potential of our independence in educational matters from Westminster, and embody some vision of how education relates to our human and societal well-being.

THE GLOBAL CONTEXT : LOCATING ENLIGHTENMENT

The historic failure of the Soviet enterprise and the current economic and political dominance of the U.S., together with the huge surge in global monetarism, find us in a situation where market economics seem axiomatic. Yet, from a Christian perspective one might want to say, 'Money was made for man, not man for money'. Indeed, as John Hull, Professor of Religious Education at Birmingham University, has been pointing out for many years, money is made *by* man.[2] It is, in the strictest sense a fiction, something to which human society, now globally interconnected, gives reality and value. The bits of metal and paper, now replaced by virtual capital, which bounce round the globe destabilising economies and toppling politicians, are not in themselves demonic. But if they become the measure of value we put on everything, and particularly on people, then we have, in old-fashioned Biblical terms, become idolatrous. This is not the place for an essay in alternative economics, even were I capable of it. But as we equip our children to function in the existing world, we are also needing to educate them to question our axioms; to hear voices like that of Vandana Shiva, who in last year's Reith Lectures detailed the negative impact of global economics on the culture of the Indian villages around her. Too one-sided perhaps, but an awareness of a question which is vital if the coming generation is to participate in real decision-making about the kind of world we want.

Of course, there are certain 'givens', functions of cosmology, space, time, causality, with which, for good or ill, we are landed. In addition we have, perhaps increasingly, capacities to intervene, most conspicuously as the understanding of genetics accelerates. I am not in the least supposing that here lies a magic solution to various aspects of the human predicament: indeed I think we must beware of 'hubris', of thinking we can blueprint a mechanically engineered salvation of any area of human life. But I am quite sure that the Christian faith does not support either an uncritical veneration of nature as it is, nor any kind of political or economic or biological determinism.

What we need to offer our children, and our adults who have not received it as children, is the chance to appreciate reality in all its complexity, and not to be daunted by it. Schooling, of course, is merely a fraction of the educational experience a young person has. Learning goes on, usually more intimately, in the context of family, of parenting, of sibling encounter, of playing with peers. But it is, increasingly, formal educational qualifications which count for work opportunities, and for social prestige. And there is a pecking order of esteem which cannot be disguised by the expedient of universal certification. League tables have gone into our souls.

LEARNING FOR LIVING : MARKS OF ENLIGHTENMENT

'Appreciating reality in all its complexity' is a spiritual exercise, and a collaborative one. It involves much more than registering data. It challenges us to make value judgments, commitments of will and energy and emotional engagements. No one can do it starting from scratch, though in another sense, everyone has to do it for him or her self, through the integrity of his or her own experience and reflection. What is made available within our corporate culture will affect the possibilities. A home in which there is never silence; a classroom in which there is only a concern for cognitive outcomes; a media culture in which only 'spin' is anticipated – such factors will be seriously destructive of wholesome education.

Children have a natural capacity for wonder: watch a baby in a pram under a tree. But if they are introduced for the first few years into the stress and neglect and violence and bleakness of some of our urban ghettos or the mindless consumerism so vital for capitalist growth, they are likely to enter school already severely handicapped. They have a natural capacity for affection. But if they have spent their early childhood with carers too preoccupied with survival to build their self-esteem; or in contexts where adults represent only power and violence, the remedial action needed within formal education will be colossal. Citizenship – one of the latest demands on the curriculum – is almost a laughable objective for children who live in our drug-ridden concrete jungles of mass unemployment and compensatory addiction. At the other end of the social scale, what human values are likely to emerge from a school whose 'enterprise magazine' advocates tidiness and decorum in the neighbourhood, because that is likely to enhance house prices!?

Paulo Freire's 'Pedagogy of the Oppressed' classically recognised the impotence of what he called 'banking education' to overcome socio-economic political alienation, and to act as a real force for liberation. Education at its best is a way of breaking the 'culture of silence' by allowing people to 'perceive, interpret, criticise and transform the world about them'.

John Hull identifies a similar alternative between 'a curriculum for life' and a 'curriculum for death'.[3] It is not enough to inject into the overall programme of a school little slots for 'citizenship' or 'spirituality'. If there are directions of the spirit which are creative and life-giving they have to be addressed as much in the teaching of Geography or Technology as in the Personal and Social Education or the Religious and Moral Education slots; as much in the methodology of teaching and learning as in the content; as well in the ethos and 'informal curriculum' of the school as in its timetabled activities.

What Professor Graham calls 'enrichment' is well documented in third section of his paper, in the university context. At the school level, I would argue that it is a primary responsibility of education to be concerned about these 'whole-person' and 'whole-community' values, which will generate the flavour of our society. I have already named the capacity for 'wonder' as one of the things which can be knocked out of children by bad schooling. There are several others.

- ◆ The capacity for disinterested attention: Noticing things for themselves, not for 'what's in it for you'. (Simone Weil in 'Waiting for God' says important things about all education as preparation for attention to God.)
- ◆ The capacity for making connections: An increasingly atomised curriculum leaves young people at risk of finding it harder to see links between what they learn in History and what they learn in Biology. Or what they do in French lessons and their own needs and desires to communicate and be communicated with.
- ◆ The capacity for critical reflection: This includes the development of questioning attitudes, the ability to compare different situations and different responses to them; the confidence to challenge received opinion.

◆ The initial integration of work and play: In the best stretch of education my children ever had, which was in their nursery school period, play was the vehicle for working and learning. By Primary One, play was a reward for having done work; an alternative to work. So the feel of play is deeply important and creative and world-sustaining, whether it be with words or the stuff of creation is lost, and play is trivialised to 'relaxation' and 'amusement' or 'fun'. 'Work' on the other hand was the serious stuff to be done with intensity and concentration, measured and tested, whether by gold stars or formal grades. The idea of the root etymology of scholarship as 'schole' – leisure; of it involving wandering as well as wondering is submerged, sometimes never to return. Learning becomes a utilitarian, targeted process, not a matter of delight and exploration.

THREATS TO ENLIGHTENMENT

We are not lacking in educational documents which express concern for whole person education, though I think we have almost lost from public discourse the idea of education as a subversive discipline, which was certainly one element in the Enlightenment protest against bigotry, authoritarianism, cant and obscurantism. There are 'social clonings' afoot no less sinister than genetic ones in which conformism to the dominant social values, even if these include a superficial 'individualism', which threaten the genuine diversity and variety of human community. The growing pressure on both parents to work for money whether they will or not (in earlier feminism a right to fight for, but for many now a cause of huge malaise and of sheer economic necessity) is one such trend: the lack of role models for the young who resist or challenge from within the 'bread and circuses' tie up between wealth and entertainment; the almost irresistible sexualisation, particularly of girls, by the fashion industry; the monopolistic and ratings-orientated packaging of news; the corruption of libraries, market-driven, to purveyors of 'popular' shelves of crimes, romance, travel and D.I.Y., as well as drastic cuts in opening hours; all these things assault the freedom and integrity of many. Brilliant educational experiments, like Canada's admission of retired people to free higher education, have been squeezed out by market-force economics. Indeed the elderly may become the next group who have to justify their existence by on-going 'economic viability'. (Some want to, but should they need to?) The potential of inter-generational life for exploring 'wisdom', so powerful formerly in traditional societies, is likely to be replaced by the sense of cosmic access to information. It was pointed out to me a few months ago that a youngster now can surf, in a week, more data than his grandparents could in a lifetime. But is that knowledge?

What is different from the classic Enlightenment of Western Europe is that we now inhabit a world in which the historic and contemporary plurality of values, cultures, ethics and lifestyles is manifest. We can name the imperialisms of white, upper class, rationalist, scientist society. We even apologise for some of them, and scramble for restitution through our investments in indigenous cultures, our fascination with holistic spiritualities, and our 'back to nature' agendas. (We do not, however, often ask whether the 'knowledge' economy is simply the latest form of such imperialism, merely overlaid by surface contrition.)

Enlightenment today would have to be about how to handle the Babel/babble of voices, ideologies, programmes of self-improvement, emotional fragmentations which characterise the post-modern world. If that is to avoid the double risks of laissez-faire indifferentism ('You have God; I'll have aromatherapy myself.'), or of totalitarianism (the rise of fundamentalism in many religious cultures), we are desperately in need of life-long learning strategies which might help us develop a real, open, listening dialogue of cultures. If we allow our education systems in fact to serve the monoculture of the market, we will signally fail to do that.

The churches, of course, are themselves involved in that monoculture. We too are tempted to appraise ourselves by measurable results, to quantify the "success" of ministry, to value congregations by their cost-effectiveness, to ape the world in 'marketing' Christianity, to see other faiths as competitors. We are not conspicuous bearers of emotional literacy to children, or to wounded adults. (They flock rather to the therapeutic professions which do not disclose their dogmatic involvements.) We are not conspicuous as questioners of political compromise, though there are flurries of activity on personal/social/sexual issues; we hardly model the flowering of imaginative life in our churchy publications, or the encouragement of critical questioning in our catechetics or adult education (except in tiny patches). If we did those things, we would be a significant counter-culture, bearers of real enlightenment.

OUR VOCATION : MODELLING ENLIGHTENMENT

Someone who is employed full-time by one of the Scottish churches expressed the judgment some months ago that most thinking people had already left the church. I hope he is wrong, for I believe that it is part of our vocation to model a community that shows what 'fullness of life' looks like, and that involves the creation of structures of mutuality, of participation, of truthfulness, of accountability which energise and stretch our members. It also involves an invitation and a challenge to the world to recognise elements of the human birthright in creation –

- ◆ That the world is wondrous, and that its celebration involves the gifts of science and art and all the modes of apprehension available to us;
- ◆ That there are things which cannot be measured, some of them most precious and which have no monetary exchange value;
- ◆ That the planet and its inhabitants are fragile and inter-connected, so that what we do or fail to do in stewardship will affect the quality of life of our whole future;
- ◆ That humans are endowed for that stewardship with faculties of caring, intelligence, imagination and will;
- ◆ That the fullness of our humanity is grotesquely altered if we are reduced to economic functionaries, either in work or in leisure;
- ◆ That the glories and horrors of being human teach us how little we are self-sufficient, and how much inter-dependent.

How we would get from here to there is not a matter of facile blueprinting. At the end of a few millennia of 'civilisation', we are still infants in creating the kind of listening to one another, to the earth, and to the 'beyond earth' reality which faith traditions in diverse ways worship as holy.

But to long to get there, to insist that public resources need to be spent on such a birthright, that people need to be equipped to articulate it and treasure it, that all need access to it – that would be an enlightenment worth spelling out in costly educational, political and economic detail. To put corporate energy into such a task would be to break genuinely new ground.

CHAPTER THREE

BREAKING FREE FROM ALIENATION

Racism, Migration and Asylum

Mukami McCrum

INTRODUCTION

One of the blessings human beings possess is the ability to dream, to imagine and to visualise a better future. The notion of breaking new ground, which means doing something that has not been done before, fills me with a deep sense of hope and promise, a hope, borne of expectations that a new beginning will bring new benefits. The possibility of making new ideas work, the challenge of overcoming barriers and the thrill of discovery generates hope and a sense of purpose. It is as exciting as setting out on a journey of exploration to the unknown. It is a time for renewal – as spring renews life after winter. It also raises a number of questions. What if there are no new grounds to break? Suppose that there are no more final frontiers and boundaries to cross? Why do we want to break new grounds?

In gardening terms, when the soil is tired and no longer yields a good harvest, it is time for the gardener to seek new ways of improving the crop. It may involve moving to a completely new patch or looking for ways to make the soil fertile again. But when there is no more land within reach, what are the alternatives? It could be that new tools are needed or old ones sharpened.

In the context of *racism, migration and asylum*, the ways we treat each other, and the widespread nature of bigotry, conflicts and hatreds, have destabilised the relationship between nations and peoples of the world today. These have reached a crisis point that threatens the core of our humanity. Something has to be done and done immediately. The greatest threat to peace and well being comes from oppressive and hostile relationships between people as individuals, as members of the family or community, and as nations. The world cannot afford to go on being divided by poverty, bigotry, violence, and wars. More and more people now agree that it is time to find new ways of overcoming the oppression that is so clearly threatening peace.

There is a tendency to look at any form of *oppression*, and in particular racism, in terms of black and white. There are those who see the world as essentially divided between black and white, and status is accorded to individuals depending on the tone of the colour of the skin. In this view, all people who have white or fair skin colour, and who are mostly of European origin, are perceived to be better and superior. The people who have dark skins are perceived to be inferior, oppressed or the dispossessed ones. Their origins tend to be from African or Asian continents, or Indigenous People from the Americas, Australia and other countries from the south. To complicate matters, all white people are seen as the oppressors from rich and developed countries, and they are also attributed with positive qualities: good, virtuous, clean, rational, civilised, godly, moral, close to heaven. Black is linked with the oppressed and characterised by negative qualities: evil, criminal, and heathen, irrational and primitive and animal-like in nature, demonic, immoral. While these terms are dated, they influence many aspects of personal and collective relationships, at work, in residential areas, in streets and public places, and sadly, even within the places of worship. This view of the world creates a divided humanity and ends with a divided world, which makes a mockery of the term 'one world', except in the minds of those who are working towards breaking the barriers.

This is a simplistic and dangerous way of looking at discrimination. It creates a bipolar paradigm and fails to make the links between different forms of oppression – gender, class, and disability – and furthermore, it overlooks wars, ethnic conflicts and xenophobia that can occur within communities of people of the same colour. The two World Wars and more recently the genocide in Bosnia, Chechnya, Sierra Leone and Rwanda were conflicts between people of the same colour. Bipolar models inevitably rely on simple explanations that create monsters and angels, conquerors and conquered victims and perpetrators, oppressors and oppressed. Looking at racism or any form of discrimination in simplistic terms widens the gap and perpetuates the myths and stereotypes that dehumanise people. It is worthwhile trying to understand how these perceptions are formed and perpetuated.

Fear of one another is a powerful force that drives people into irrational and unexplainable behaviour towards one another. As opposing sides become more and more entrenched, they pass their views about the inferiority or inhumanity of the other, from generation to generation through laws, education, culture, music, literature, art and the media. They reject and resist any opportunity to look at the problem from their opponents' perspective and over a period of time, their beliefs become embedded in their psyche to such an extent that acts of racism and xenophobia are perceived as normal and inevitable ways of life. In the absence of sanctions, when prejudice is combined with power and an opportunity to discriminate, a great evil is unleashed on earth.

These opposing views heighten the struggle by dividing victims and causing bitter arguments between those who promote the term '*black*' as a political identity, and those who reject it on the grounds that their colour does not have a dark pigmentation. Others claim the moral ground because their skin colour has made them victims of racial oppression and exploitation. Both schools of thought are problematic to those who pursue justice on the ground of human rights based on the premise that there is only one human race. Furthermore, in terms of identity, as Africans in Scotland[1] have pointed out many times, colour coding people is immoral and unjustifiable in this century. The terms *black and white* have no biological, racial, ethnic, or religious validity. They merely describe what people are (i.e. look like) but not who they are, and thus ignore the diversity of the human race. Under such circumstances, change is very difficult if not impossible. However, there is an alternative view – a view promoted by people on both sides of the divide who believe in human rights, equality, fairness and justice.

A significant omission in this equation is the large number of people in both camps who experience particular forms of oppression, and more importantly, those who do not subscribe to the bipolar models. Powerlessness, poverty, disability, gender and age oppression affect people regardless of their colour or creed. These are the people who are willing to work for peace and 'break new ground' to bridge the gap and close the divide. Our hope lies in the hands of such people who cross the boundaries and change the world by challenging and resisting the status quo.

Ironically, issues concerning migration, asylum and racism are about people who have attempted to break new grounds by following their dreams and visions of new and better beginnings. In so doing, they place their lives in danger as they attempt to cross boundaries and climb over barriers that are becoming increasingly difficult to overcome. Gates, walls and fortresses they encounter on the way become bigger, higher and more impregnable as the rest of the world uses more sophisticated methods to keep newcomers out. Those who are rich and powerful deny the poor and the dispossessed the powerful and energising message of hope that comes from 'breaking new ground'. Their hopes are dashed on the rocks of oppression and persecution, of injustice and marginalisation, of destruction and war, and of the sin and obscenity of racism, xenophobia and violence, at the hands of other human beings.

Uprooted people experience violence and persecution across ethnic, racial and religious lines. The consequences of their oppression is the disruption of their lives, their family ties and their communities. They suffer from broken relationships and from the refusal of the settled people to share space and land with them. Without adequate hospitable habitat people cannot live. This is not only the case for humans; all life forms require particular space and habitat carefully fitted for them in the household of life.

RACISM – A BARRIER TO PEACE

Over the years definitions of racism have changed, evolving from the direct experience and manifestations of racism at specific periods in history and in different societies and countries. In the 21st century, the greatest challenges facing mankind have been summarised as eliminating poverty, halting environmental degradation and managing human diversity. *The previous secretary general of the Commonwealth, Chief Emeka Anyaoku, says that it is not just a challenge of resolving conflicts between long-settled peoples in their own lands, but also of defusing racial hostility towards new immigrant minorities moving from the poor developing countries of the south to the wealthy industrialised nations of the north.* The ideology of white superiority has had strong prevalence in all parts of the world and it is strongly linked to other global challenges such as migration and poverty. It is not a coincidence that the poorest countries are in the south, in countries that are predominantly inhabited by non-Europeans and people who have been subjected to inhumane treatment because of their colour.

A simple definition states that 'racism exists when one group of people assumes superiority and treats other groups of people as inferior because of their colour, ethnicity, cultural and racial grounds'. The reference to racial groups implies that there is more than one human race. Although there is no biological basis for this suggestion, the early definitions of racism were based on experiences of people who were discriminated against because of their physical characteristics including colour, language, culture, and religion. This treatment may have its roots in the past, but the world we live in today legitimises and perpetuates racism on the same lines. It is therefore, imperative that all definitions should take into account the perceptions and experiences of the victims and not the justifications of the perpetrator. Although there is a lack of consensus about definitions and terminology among the people who experience racism, most of the definitions in current use, and which have survived the test of time, are based on the principles laid down in the UN Conventions for the Protection of Human Rights.

International Conventions and Declarations for the elimination of racism and intolerance focus on the definition of 'racial discrimination' and not that of racism. This leads to a broad based definition which focuses on attitudes and prejudice and ignores the specific nature of racism characterised by repression and violence in the form of verbal and physical attacks, rape, arson, murder and damage to property. Broad definitions also ignore the role power plays to enforce, entrench and legitimise prejudice that leads to racism. In recent times new definitions have arisen out of the specific experiences of conflicts between different ethnic groups, wars and internal conflicts and xenophobia.

The Declaration on the Elimination of All Forms of Racial Discrimination, 20 Nov. 1963 states that, '*Discrimination between human beings on the grounds of race, colour or ethnic origin is an offence to human dignity and shall be condemned as a denial of the principles of the Charter of the United Nations, as a violation of the human rights and fundamental freedoms proclaimed in the Universal Declaration of Human Rights, as an obstacle to friendly and peaceful relations among nations and as a fact capable of disturbing peace and security among peoples*'.

Article 1 of the International Convention on the Elimination of all Forms of Racial Discrimination which came into effect a few years later, further states that, 'In this Convention, the term '*Racial Discrimination*' shall mean any distinction, exclusion, restriction or preference based on race, colour, descent, or national or ethnic origin which has the purpose or effect of nullifying or impairing the recognition, enjoyment or exercise, on an equal footing, of human rights and fundamental freedoms in the political, economic social, cultural or any other field of public life'.

In the UK, the Race Relations Act 1976 promoted by the Commission for Racial Equality (CRE) defines two forms of racial discrimination. *Direct Discrimination* is when a person is treated less favourably than others, on the ground of race, colour, nationality, citizenship, ethnic origin or national origin. *Indirect Discrimination* occurs when a rule or policy puts people in from a particular racial group at a much greater disadvantage than others.

The most reported form of racism is *Racial Harassment* which is defined as follows: 'Any incidents, which involve actions or threats which are perceived by the complainer or any other person, as having a racial motivation. This may include verbal abuse, physical attack, assault, damage to property, graffiti, rude gestures, bullying, and in extreme cases, murder'.

Following the Inquiry into the murder of Stephen Lawrence, the term *institutional racism* was defined as: 'The collective failure of an organisation to provide an appropriate and professional service to people because of their colour, culture or ethnic origin. It can be seen or detected in processes, attitudes and behaviour which amount to discrimination through unwitting prejudice, ignorance, thoughtlessness and racist stereotyping which disadvantage minority ethnic people'.

New forms of intolerance have been named over the last 50 years, since the Universal Declaration of Human Rights. To refer to them as newly emerged forms of racism is erroneous given the fact that they existed alongside, but were masked by, other forms of oppression which united old adversaries to resist a common and shared form of oppression such as colonialism, dictatorship, sectarian and religious persecution. Later, when political independence was won, power struggle, poverty, unequal social and economic status unleashed the old sentiments of prejudices and fears. Racism is not just about prejudice and power; it is about the struggle for economic resources, political power, and social status of diverse groups of people. Throughout history, people who are different because of culture, religion, language or a long shared history have fought each other for domination and control.

THE DESTRUCTIVENESS OF RACISM

Racism damages everyone who experiences it in many ways. Sometimes the damage is hidden but the consequences to the victims are quite clear when examined in comparison with the lives of those who do not experience it. It must not be confused with other forms of oppression such as gender or class. Although they may have the same effects on the health, peace and well-being of people, their roots are different and therefore they demand different responses. The damage that racism can cause is best understood in terms of what it does to people, psychologically, physically, and economically.

Literature, especially from the Caribbean and Americas, reveals the complexity of the lives of the descendants of slaves who were taken from Africa. The status, privileges and experiences of the different ethnic groups in the region are still determined by the shade of their skin colour and by the reasons for their migration to the region. Europeans went as explorers, settlers and plantation owners, and therefore as the 'masters' occupying the top strata of society and controlling the political, economic and military power. They were bestowed with privileges and opportunities to control and rule the Africans who were taken there as slaves, and the Asians who went as indentured labourers. The colour *black* was then, as now, associated with negative connotations of inferiority and crime and, at best, accorded lower status as human beings and, at worst, treated worse than animals without a soul. The colour *black* was also a justification for violence (murder, beatings, lynching, and rape), atrocities, and inhumane treatment of slaves. In today's context, Dr Nyameko Barney Pityana, referring to the South African situation, argues that *'the equation of blackness with corruption, inefficiency, and other forms of criminal conduct, have become so commonplace that we are in danger of accepting it as fact or a matter of course'*. Consequently, on one level, it affects the way people perceive themselves in relation to others, and makes children grow up with distorted views and images of themselves. On another level, it destroys the relationships between people, as individuals, ethnic groups and as nations.

Racism is also damaging and harmful to human beings at the individual and collective level. Centuries of racism have *left psychological* scars on victims which sometimes linger on from generation to generation affecting adversely their sense of belonging, identity and self esteem. When the social, cultural and religious identity of people is deemed to be of lower status, it affects the people, especially those who do not become assimilated into, or readily adopt, the values, characteristics and way of life of the dominant group. To belong to a group of people who are oppressed, diminishes the collective capacity and the power to achieve and participate on an equal footing in life and in decision making. Associating black with negative connotations has made some people dislike their colour and led them to take drastic steps to change it. Unfortunately, colour is not easily disguised and damage is often irreversible and further erodes the status of racially oppressed people, as is the case in 'the 'whitening' of music, literature, art and science to make them acceptable; the difficulties experienced by people from mixed parentage who try to pass as white; the struggles of women scientists, authors and doctors who disguise their gender in order to work in a field dominated by male opinion. The following examples show that this is not a new concern.

◆ In the book titled *Passing* first published in 1928; Nella Larsen describes the sad experiences of black people who go to great lengths to hide the fact that in their distant past their roots have mixed parentage. They live their lives as white people for economic and social gain but also live in fear of being found out. The book highlights the emotional confusion arising from denial of one's identity, parallelled today by the psychological effects of low esteem and lack of confidence caused by lack of a true sense of belonging.

◆ 'Whitening' the race, as in the case of Trujillo (a dictator between 1930 and 1960) who encouraged the immigration of white people, whom he considered superior in the belief that whitening the Dominican people would be better for the race.

◆ There are chilling stories about black children who, after getting tired of being teased, bullied and excluded by their white peers, used bleach in an attempt to whiten their skin.

◆ Some mothers have told, with tears in their eyes, how their children would wear, balaclavas, straw hats or hide indoors during the summer to avoid the sun in case they get darker from exposure to the sun.

◆ In Africa, and some parts of UK, some women will buy highly toxic skin bleaching[2] products in the name of beauty. Sadly, a few shopkeepers will exploit this misguided vanity and sell forbidden products under the counter.

◆ There was a time when some foster parents used the 'hair test' to identify the children who had African ancestry. In this case they would rub the child's head, supposedly to show affection but they were actually testing the texture of the hair. As a result the African or Caribbean children were the most difficult to place with foster parents.

Low self esteem and lack of confidence has a dreadful effect on young people growing up under any form of racism. They are criminalised from birth by virtue of being born to a particular group of people and this stigma follows them throughout their life in education, employment and personal relationships. In any encounter with the state or the law enforcement forces, they come out worst. Recent research on exclusion from school has shown that black children are excluded, apparently for bad behaviour, when in fact they have fought back after long periods of putting up with harassment and bullying while the school did nothing.

Living in fear of racist violence is damaging to physical and mental health. It impacts on every aspect of life adding stress to the lives of people who are already burdened by other stresses of daily living, such as unemployment. This remains one of the most terrifying experiences for black people in many cities and towns in Britain. Innocent people, irrespective of their nationality or citizenship, are physically attacked, insulted or threatened simply because of their colour, ethnicity, origin, religion or because they appear to be foreign. The brutality and viciousness of these unprovoked attacks varies in seriousness and ranges from murder, at the one extreme, through shooting and stabbing, to beatings, punching, kicking, arson, bullying, insults and name calling, at the other extreme. In the British Crime Survey Report March 2000, ethnic minority people scored higher than the white majority population in all measurements of fear of crime. They perceive themselves to be at greater risk of crime, worry more about falling victim of crime and feel less safe in the streets and in their homes at night. The percentage of those who are worried about racial attacks is as follows:- white 7%; black 27%; Indian 35%; Pakistani / Bangladeshi 38%. The report argues that this is a reflection of their higher risks of victimization. In contrast, the media, the criminal justice system and society as whole portray black and minority ethnic people as criminals.

Racism is not a new phenomenon. It has existed for centuries and it is disappointing to note that it is on the increase in every continent in the world in spite of international efforts. The response to racism varies from country to country depending on a range of factors such as the existence of legal instruments, policies and procedures as well as access to community-based support systems. It is therefore pertinent to ask why the legal instruments we have today have failed to eliminate racism and what is the next step. Many arguments are put forward including that it is natural and normal for human beings to be prejudiced. But it is important to look beyond such excuses.

In 1963 the UN General Assembly adopted the Declaration on the Elimination of all forms of Racial Discrimination which came into force in 1969. The Declaration states that racial discrimination is not only a violation of human rights and fundamental freedoms, it is an obstacle to friendly and peaceful relations among nations and as a fact capable of disturbing the peace and security among peoples.

Prior to this Convention, an earlier declaration, the Universal Declaration of Human Rights (UDHR), 1948, was the start of international co-operation on the elimination of racial discrimination. It grew out of world-wide concern about the intolerances that led to two world wars in the first half of the 20th century. The declaration that UDHR made in 1948, in the 1st Article, *that all human beings are born equal*, was the acknowledgement of the universality of human rights. However, the implementation of this declaration, and subsequent conventions was not universally applied. There has never been a total acceptance of the principles of equality and economic, political and national interests have always been prioritised over and above human rights. There have been numerous discussions, writings, conferences, seminars and summits[3] that highlight the consequences of this racism but until these principles are actively pursued, they will remain only platitudes and rhetoric.

It seems to me that some of the new policies, initiatives and laws are there merely to establish and maintain a semblance of equality, but in real terms nothing changes. We live in a world torn apart by racial bigotry and prejudice, a world that is not managing to heal the scars and bitter consequences of the slave trade, two world wars, and economic and colonial oppression. At best, there is denial of the existence of racism coupled with the defence of the status quo, and at worst, new forms of racism are constructed to reclaim the ground that has been won by campaigns against racism. Furthermore, new suggestions such as moving towards the *mainstreaming* of policies and action against oppression are problematic. They imply that a degree of success in combating racism and in empowering the marginalised and excluded people has been achieved. However, a close look at mainstream institutions reveals that the participation of ethnic minority people and communities in government and employment is minimal or non-existent. While it is true that a few men and women from racially opposed groups have broken the 'black glass ceiling'; the situation for the majority is still far from good. On the face of it, *mainstreaming* is a positive step, which demands that institutional racism is eliminated at all levels of service delivery, employment and education. Service delivery should be carried out in a fair and equal manner that takes into account individual needs and diversity. However, in the climate of denial that still exists, coupled with massive ignorance about diversity, there are serious doubts that *mainstreaming* alone will bring about the necessary change. It might work if accountability and sanctions are built in, but it will be meaningless and it risks sweeping aside the few examples of good practice that exist today. So, what is the best way forward?

MIGRATION AND ASYLUM

The terms *migrant and immigrant* evoke a variety of positive and negative reactions depending on the motive behind the use of the words. Migration at its simplest definition refers to movement of people from country to country or internally with the borders of a country. It is also used to refer to seasonal migration of birds and animals and it is interesting to note that the latter does not cause the uproar associated with movement of people. On the contrary, television programmes about animals trekking long distances in search of food and water evoke wonderful feelings among many people. In spring and autumn one sees people gazing skywards with a smile as they watch birds fly past. In both cases, human and animal migrations are driven by a natural desire for – and a right to – adequate and hospitable habitat. Migration is therefore about survival and it is not a new thing. People have moved in search of better and safe places to live since the dawn of history. What has changed is the way the world responds to the human crisis of today. Until last century, human beings had the free run of the world and the main barriers were the weather and topography, which were easily overcome with ingenuity. Before the First World War, in most countries including the UK, people were able to move without any restriction. Even after the first Alien Act was passed in 1905, people from the Commonwealth had the right of abode in the UK. However, the situation changed later and it is the post-war migration that is the issue today and this begs the question 'why?'

The root causes of recent migration and displacement of people are well documented: war, politics, persecution, environment and economic advantage. Inevitably the people on the move are those who are affected or threatened by adverse conditions and who fear for their safety, such as refugees and asylum seekers. Unfortunately, they are defined and given status by people who live under quite the opposite circumstances. Recently, there has been a tendency to divide the people on the move into categories of those who deserve support and those who do not qualify. Some of them are accused of being bogus or economic migrants and therefore not proper refugees. Does this mean that it is okay to die from hunger, disease and poor environment as long as there are no bullets involved? It is not appropriate to discuss migration without including all people who are concerned and without understanding the contexts in which they move, such as prevailing and growing social and political racism. People who are alienated must be allowed to define the nature of their alienation and take part in finding solutions.

Pressure to migrate has increased as the political and economic situation in many countries has deteriorated. At the same time global, social, economic problems, which are closely linked to political crises have forced more black and ethnic minority people from the developing countries to flee tyranny, persecution, conflict, violence, hunger and disease. In 1995 it was estimated that 1 in 50 people lived outside their country of origin; that 80 % of refugees were women; and that there were 15 million recognised refugees and 30 million displaced people in the world. Recent political conflicts in different countries have increased fear and poverty, and the situation and statistics have changed for the worse. The UN High Commission on Refugees (UNHCR) figures for the 'people of concern'[4] are increasing as the figures below indicate. At the start of the new millennium the number of people of concern to UNHCR was 22.3 million. This is equal to one out of every 269 persons on Earth. This compared with the 1 January 1999 figure of 21.5 million. The conflicts in Kosovo and the Balkan region were largely responsible for the latest increase. While the overall number of people helped by UNHCR rose by more than one million in Europe during the year, the figures in all other areas of the world, including Africa, Asia, Latin America and the Caribbean, North America and Oceania, dropped slightly.

As the pressure to move increases, the receiving countries, especially in the north, take measures to keep newcomers out. Receiving countries are portrayed as innocent bystanders who are being overrun by hordes of people knocking at their doors. In 1992 the Single European Act (SEA) came into effect. Its main aim was to create a single and exclusive market for Europeans by further restricting the movement of people from outside. Recent major changes in British policies with regard to refugees, asylum seekers, immigration controls (internal and external checks), welfare benefits and legal aid were designed in line with the aims of SEA. The 1996 Asylum and Immigration Act created massive problems for asylum seekers and resident black people, it fuelled racist and xenophobic sentiments in a shocking and unprecedented manner. The Asylum and Immigration Act 1998 has tightened the laws further.

POVERTY: NORTH-SOUTH DIVIDE

World economics, poverty and the *North-South Divide* play a major part in the movement of people. People from the north find it easier to move to the south for pleasure or as expatriates but the reverse is not the case. The prediction Chief Emeka Anyaoku made has come true. He said that, next to the challenge of managing diversity, the second great source of tension would be that of the *North-South Divide*. The U.N. recognises that the gap has got wider even as the world as a whole has become more prosperous. Thirty years ago, the gap between the richest fifth of the world's people and the poorest stood at 30 to 1. By 1990 it had widened to 60 to 1 and today it stands at 74 to 1. In terms of consumption, the richest fifth account for 86% while the bottom fifth account for just 1%. With globalisation in mind, he felt that the combination of poverty and ever increasing information flows might prove to be an explosive mixture. The better educated in regions such as the Indian sub-continent and North Africa will be tempted to migrate in increasing numbers to Europe and the US. Last year, Germany and UK sought computer and IT experts from India. This has raised concerns about the brain drain from the sending countries, and hostile reactions from right wing elements of the receiving countries. The only way to stem the movement of people is to stop exploitation and to bring economic development and benefits to the rural areas and to the south.

Linked to poverty, the third great challenge will be to ensure that the combination of *advancing technology, material consumption and population do not leave the world environmentally uninhabitable*. The challenge for the next millennium will be to ensure that the advances of science and technology, of medicine, and human knowledge, do not divide and eventually impoverish the world. If all the technological advances are concentrated in rich and comfortable nations, the world is likely to become a less stable place, instead of a more peaceful and prosperous world. There are indications that poor people, especially women, are lagging behind and not benefiting from this technological advance. Richard Jolly[5] said, 'We must bring human development and social protection into the equation.' Breakthroughs like the Internet can offer a fast track to growth, but at present only the rich and educated benefit. Of the net's users, 88% live in the west, says the report, adding: 'The literally well connected have an overpowering advantage over the unconnected poor whose voices and concerns are being left out of the global agenda.' In developing countries, the necessary infrastructure is not available. Almost 75% of the world's telephone lines – essential for new technologies like the net – are in the west, yet it has just 17% of the world's population.

Disproportionate wealth and economic development encourage migrant workers to move from rural zones to cities in developing countries. There is pressure on land as population increases. There is environmental degradation as a result of the promise of employment and easier life in cities and towns. Even with all this in mind, those who benefit from globalisation continue to push forward the argument that liberalisation of trade, free trade and free movement of capital will benefit the poor. However, the UN disagrees with the notion that deregularised markets will bring benefits and argues that poverty, inequality and insecurity have increased in the world since globalisation was launched. As poverty and insecurity increase, more people will either be forced to move or flee. Globalisation has to be put to the service of all mankind but William Pfaff, in the International Herald Tribune, July 2000, argues that globalisation as a tool for eliminating poverty has failed. People in the industrial countries are now 74 times richer than those in the poorest. The wealth of the three richest men in the world is greater than the combined GNP of all of the least developed countries totalling 600 million people. This impoverishment has occurred at a time when globalisation was supposed to have launched the poor into sustained economic growth. It has done nothing of the kind!

HOSTILITIES: There are other concerns and difficulties facing the migrants who manage to enter the *fortress*. Both documented and undocumented workers face racism and *hostilities* from the state and on the streets. They are not entitled to the same basic necessities as the citizens of the host country and receive less welfare benefits than the local people. Attempts to supplement their income take them to areas of work where they are likely to be exploited and unfairly treated. They are low paid and often receive threats of deportation. They have no employment rights and often do the 3D jobs – *dirty, dangerous and difficult*. Women face additional gender-based difficulties. A specific example of hostility to newcomers is the murder of Axmed Shek, a Somali refugee, who was murdered in Edinburgh in 1989.

TRAFFICKING: The trafficking of people has become a lucrative business among the criminals. The stories women tell about their experiences are horrific but the reality is often worse. Trafficking is defined as the process by which women are taken into prostitution, marriage or domestic service through an agent or bureau that acts as a third party. Trafficking is a specific form of exploitation of women, often with direct financial benefits for the agents or bureau involved in the deal. Women are not the only people used for trafficking. People who need jobs but are not able to enter Europe by legitimate routes, fall into the hands of illegal labour bureaux at a very high cost. If they manage to get in, they must live in hiding. Like women they are open to abuse and threats. It is difficult for people who have never gone through poverty or fear for their lives to understand why people would go to such lengths to get into safer countries. Last year, 58 young Chinese men died from suffocation in the back of a lorry as they travelled across Europe en route to UK. Young men and boys are also victims of trafficking for the sex industry. The consequences for individuals, families and society are grave. Total denial of liberty and the rights that others take for granted is extremely painful. The issue of trafficking in women is complex and sensitive. It is about women's real life experience, which is often horrifying and life threatening, and in all aspects the reality is often more serious than the stories the women tell. It is not their chosen career and like all people on the move they dream of a better future.

ASYLUM: As stated earlier there is a connection between asylum seeking and migration in terms of the reasons and experiences. As in migration, there are specific issues for women but until recently the gender neutrality of the policies and conventions masked them. Recent immigration laws have created categories of people who are not allowed to claim asylum status because they come from countries deemed to be safe and listed on the government's 'white list'.

The few asylum seekers who make it to Europe run a gauntlet of abuse, discrimination, harassment and rejection. Their reasons for leaving are completely overlooked, which is unforgivable, considering that the West has a lot to answer for in this regard. Racists do not differentiate between refugees and other minority groups. Attacks are on colour or racial grounds, not on grounds of the immigration status of the victim. According to CRE, for 1996/97 the police recorded 13,581 racial incidents for England and Wales and 811 for Scotland. In 1999, CRE requested assistance in 1,624 cases of racial discrimination. It is estimated that due to under-reporting these figures represent only a third of incidents, which range from verbal abuse, arson, damage to property, serious assault, murder and others.

The role of the media in maligning collectively the character of refugees and ethnic minority people, and its role in distorting and misrepresenting the reality of the refugee situation, is a point worth thinking about. It masks the historical and geo-political factors for short-term economic and political gain, and incites long term hostility and antagonism towards asylum seekers. This denies people who are already vulnerable, the safety and protection proclaimed in various UN conventions. Migrants, refugees and asylum seekers are dynamic people who try very hard to stay alive. This struggle takes its toll on their mental and physical health, due to living in fear and isolation. Those who previously had an active life suffer from being cut off from participation in decision making.

A FEW SUGGESTIONS

◆ More effective use of existing legal instruments[6] is essential. We already have enough tools, but we must seek ways of making them work more effectively. The Race Relations Amendment Act 2000 came into force in April 2001. It strengthens the existing Act in two major ways: first, it extends protection against racial discrimination; second, it places a new enforceable positive duty on public authorities to promote racial equality. However, its success will depend on commitment from every one involved.

◆ Acceptance of diversity is essential[7]. Young children, from a very early age, identify the different shades of skin colour that human beings have. They do this in the same way they identify different colours in nature – animals, flowers and plants – and also artificial colours. The most significant point is that they do not attach values in comparative terms. They will comfortably approach another child or adult of different colour and touch their skin and hair. They will do this with innocence and honesty just as they would pick a flower or touch a pet as part of their leaning and understanding of their world. It is only when adults teach them about the difference, either by showing fear or distaste that the children internalise the negative aspects of the difference.

◆ Anti-racist education will shift gear from the weak multicultural approach (which has failed to shift attitudes and the balance of power) and become more radical. Racism is not just the result of ignorance of other people's culture. It is about refusing to accept diversity on equal terms. The ideology has been entrenched in society over a long time, maintained by social and political institutions, and clearly a few sessions of learning about other cultures has not changed many attitudes. Anti-racist education on the other hand, is not about workshops but about incorporating the principles of equality in the system and in people's daily lives. The aims of education for social change is to deconstruct society by addressing taboos, lies, myths and negatives images that we have internalised, and which are now being passed on to new generations. It is not about putting new policies on old frameworks or patching an old garment with a new piece of cloth.

◆ The ecumenical movement must continue to share the responsibility for engendering change, and lead the way by standing in solidarity with the oppressed.

◆ Speaking out against racial discrimination and harassment of ethnic minorities, refugees and asylum seekers is not a very popular occupation but it must be done. In Scotland now, we have a Parliament and an Executive that is accessible and committed to listening to the people. The churches should take part in any dialogues about equality, and, when necessary, initiate action to create a fair and just society.

◆ Pro-activity must be the keyword. Far too often people wait on the sidelines as if they are not part of the system. We need 'watchers' and people who are aware of the system to monitor the implementation of policies and lobby for action as necessary.

◆ Taking risks is part of 'Breaking New Ground'. We must move from our safe places and face different challenges.

◆ Commitment to the ten affirmations of Theology of Life. 'Theology of Life' is an ecumenical study based on The Affirmations of the World Convocation on Justice and Peace and Integrity of Creation held in Seoul, Korea in 1990. The study process will build on the ten affirmations in the local contexts. Three main aims are to bridge diversities through dialogue and mutual challenge; to give contemporary voice to Christian social thought and practice; and to strengthen the bases for common Christian action. *The ten affirmations are*:

1   All exercise of power is accountable to God.
2   God's option for the poor.
3   The equal value of all races and peoples.
4   That the male and female are created equal.
5   That truth is at the foundation of a community of free people.
6   We affirm the peace of Jesus Christ.
7   The creation as beloved of God.
8   That the earth is the Lord's.
9   The dignity and commitment of younger people.
10   That human rights are given by God.

NB The theology of life is a programme of World Council of Churches. The themes are central to any work or initiative for 'breaking free from alienation'.

◆ Forming communities of resistance: EU countries have resources and state machinery which can be mobilised against helpless people at very short notice. The capacity to share information, co-operate and work together to strengthen their action against refugees and asylum seekers is an eye opener. Therefore, the NGOs and the churches need to form internationally co-ordinated and harmonised structures and mechanisms to challenge governments, multinationals, transnationals and financial institutions including the World Bank and the IMF, to make them accountable for their policies and actions which lead to violations of human rights. A united and harmonised forum of resistance is needed in the European Union.

◆ In the long term, it is in the interest of host countries to assist migrants, refugees or asylum seekers in a manner which would make them economically independent, so that they can pursue education, training and employment. When the time is right they will be well prepared to participate in the development of their countries when they return.

CHAPTER FOUR

BREAKING INTO A NEW UNDERSTANDING OF WORK

Making human work more human

John W. Dyce

WORK AND ITS MEANING FOR US

At the very heart of what it is to be human lies work. For most of us, it comes as an economic necessity. We work in order to earn the means by which to buy food and shelter and clothing – the very basics for existence. Yet, work has a significance for us beyond our need for earnings. It serves important social and psychological functions for us (and, in these respects, it can do so, even where work is not economically rewarded). We draw dignity and status, we form community with others, we learn, we expend energy, we contribute to society, we express solidarity, we exercise creativity, we are mentally stimulated, we extend our frontiers . . .the outcomes of engaging in work are extensive.

As Christians, we would want also to recognise that human work has a theological dimension. We are called into being in the image and likeness of God himself (Gen 1:26),[1] of God who is Creator. It must be then that our being also has this creative urge and commitment within it. We are charged with a responsibility to bring the earth under our control (Gen 1:28), to take responsibility for how the earth, with all its resources and potential, is used. This is a duty of stewardship rather than a licence to exploit. It calls us to use what we have been entrusted with, including our own self and its capacity, to continue the creative work of God. If we are servants and stewards of Christ (1 Cor 4:1), then in all things, including our labour, we are called to be 'found trustworthy' (4:2) The Bible recognises too the need for work's productivity: 'You shall eat the fruit of the labour of your hands' (Ps 128:2). The First Epistle to the Thessalonians exhorts us to 'work with (our) hands' (4:11) and Jesus' own trade as a carpenter (Mk 6:3) encourages a positive Christian view of labour. Indeed, it would appear that a poor view is taken of idleness (2 Thess 3:10). In saying this, we must be careful not to confuse 'work' with economic activity in the labour market. Socially and theologically, many engage in 'work', whether in the home or in the community, even though they are not remunerated – and such work should not be (as it has been) accorded less dignity and regard. The focus of this article will be primarily on work in the labour market sense, because we wish to address some of the issues in that context, but this does not imply that other work is less worthy of consideration.

Though Christian scripture and tradition celebrates the importance of work for human society, it does not take an idealised romantic view. The world of work can be exploitative, both of people and of natural resources. It can operate unjustly and perpetrate injustice in economic rewards and in the distribution of power (in the Old Testament, for example, we are told of the exploitation of the people of Israel by the Egyptians – Ex 1:11-14). It can deny the dignity of human beings and diminish them psychologically, socially and spiritually. It can be used as a false measure of human worth, whereby some (and their work or indeed non-involvement in the labour market) are judged to contribute less than others or at least to be worthy of a lower reward, in both economic and social terms. It forms a fundamental mechanism in a system that perpetuates inequality economically, socially, politically and internationally. It can be used even to punish and oppress. Genesis would appear to suggest that work, which had been good (2:15), *became toil* in consequence of humankind's alienation from God (3:17-19). It is when work is distanced from its true rôle as a creative, dignified, life-enhancing human activity that it ceases to be good and becomes laborious and evil. May it be that the expression (at 3:19) 'in the sweat of your face' speaks not so much of hard and energetic labour (surely not a bad thing in itself) but of the tense, anxious, harmful, demoralising, conflictual nature of some work and working conditions? It is when work bears down on people rather than uplifting them that it becomes toil. When work contributes to 'making life more human'[2], then it shares in the creative action of God.

We cannot see work in its true relation to other things, if we imagine that human beings are merely agents in a process of production, as pawns in the labour market. The words of Jesus, 'the Sabbath was made for man, not man for the Sabbath' (Mk 2:27), challenge the priorities in our perspective: 'however true it may be that man (sic) is destined for work and called to it, in the first place work is "for man" and not man "for work".'[3] Whatever other outcomes of work there may be, the most fundamental is that it contributes to the fulfilment of each person's and the community's vocation to be human, enjoying life which is abundant (Jn 10:10).

However significant a part work may play in human living, and even allowing for a broad definition of work to include voluntary and community work, it must still be recognised that life cannot be made up wholly of work. There is need for rest, for re-creational activity, for balance between work and other human 'activities'. This too may be rooted in our understanding of our sharing in the divine creative action. 'And on the seventh day God finished his work which he had done, and he rested on the seventh day from all the work which he had done. So God blessed the seventh day and hallowed it'. (Gen 2:2-3) This balance in life, between work and re-creative experiences, is part of the equilibrium that God gifts to his creation.

This placing of the human worker at the heart of our understanding of work is not to suggest that work is *only* significant in terms of fulfilment for each individual. Work has a rôle in bringing about (or frustrating) justice and prosperity, sustainable development, peace, health and much more. If we are charged to cultivate the garden of this earth (Gen 2:15), then we must be conscious of the fruits of our labours. The product of our labour is not only the reward to ourselves, financial or psychological, but the impact on our world, socially and economically.

From this brief glance at some theological considerations, we may discern certain principles that we may use as criteria in reviewing something of contemporary experience in the labour market[4].

◆ Work has potential for good and for ill and can contribute to or work against the psychological, social, spiritual and physical well-being of individuals and their communities

◆ Labour is the primary element in work – technology or capital or other factors ought to be seen to be secondary – human beings are or ought not to be the slaves of production

◆ The core values and goals of the labour market ought to be derived from an understanding of the needs of humanity rather than from economistic or materialistic perspectives

◆ The labour market is an arena in which the struggle for justice and equality takes place

◆ Life must reflect a balance between work and 'rest'

◆ While the welfare of the individual is a legitimate and essential concern of labour market practice, an over-individualistic emphasis can have a detrimental effect on others, both immediately and in the wider society (including in other parts of the world).

◆ An appraisal of work cannot be divorced from an evaluation of the products of that work and their economic, political, environmental significance.

THE CHANGING WORLD OF WORK

There is, of necessity, too little space in this article to identify more than the main trends recently in the labour market and world of employment.

Perhaps the most apparent is the changing mix in the labour market in terms of the participation of men and women. Over the last two decades, the proportion of women who are of working age who are economically active has increased from around 55% to a projected 75% in 2006. The corresponding male figures show a decline from over 90% to a little over 80%[5]. Women make up over 40% of the UK workforce and over the next decade the increase in the workforce of 1.5m will be largely due to the greater participation of women[6].

In a number of respects, however, this does not represent as significant an advance in female labour market participation as it might seem. Between 1971 and 1993, 93% of the total increase in female employment related to part-time work[7]. This is not to suggest unequivocally that part-time employment is a wholly less desirable form of participation in the labour market. Nonetheless, we ought to hear the comment that 'the belief that women *choose* part-time work for its benefit of personal flexibility is more a matter of 'employment ideology' than a conclusion based on statistical data'[8]. Insofar as women do choose part-time work, this may in part be attributable to their continuing primary responsibility for domestic tasks[9] and for the care of children[10] and elders[11]. While the phenomenon of the 'new man' who takes his share of these responsibilities has some objective reality, as there is some evidence that men are spending increased amounts of time on housework and childcare[12], this is especially during the mother's working hours[13] and may reflect a restricted range of responsibilities.

Though sex discrimination legislation, education and labour market practice have produced substantial changes in the *kind* of work that women undertake, there do remain very real differences between the nature of 'male' and 'female' employment. Around half of women in employment are within a small number of occupational sectors which have traditionally recruited from amongst women: clerical and secretarial and personal and protective services predominating. This is not to deny that there have been significant improvements in female access to professional and managerial jobs, but it is to recognise that the equality issue is not wholly won[14]. Promotional success is still hard to come by for many women; even in those professions where there are high numbers of women working, they are under-represented in the higher echelons[15]. There continues to be argument over the existence of the 'glass ceiling' which is the experience of significant numbers of women. In terms of gender differences in pay, women's earnings on average continue to be lower than those of men. Advances there have been certainly, but the greatest change was post the introduction of the equal pay legislation and progress thereafter has noticeably slowed down.

This shift towards greater female participation in the labour market has many different causes:

◆ Demographic shifts have produced a shortage of labour recruits
◆ The nature of skill demand has changed, particularly in the direction of 'feminine' industries and services
◆ Labour market needs have outstripped traditional labour market sources
◆ Women's aspirations and social rôles have changed owing to shifts in thinking and in education and cultural norms
◆ Consumerism has tended to extend demand for goods and services beyond that which can be readily afforded on a single (traditionally male) income and the 'necessity' for dual income has grown
◆ Job insecurity has made a family single income appear a risky financial strategy.

Quite readily one may identify factors which can affect the capacity of women to achieve equality within the labour market:

◆ The burden on women (however imposed) to take responsibility for child and elder care and lack of access to affordable and flexible care or working arrangements
◆ Direct or indirect discrimination
◆ The persistence of informal networks to which women have relatively poorer access
◆ A dominant male culture in many workplaces
◆ Education and support to challenge stereotypical values and assumptions
◆ Occupational segregation, whereby some jobs are thought to be more appropriate to or even restricted to particular genders
◆ Resistance to women in authority
◆ Difficulty in establishing consistent career patterns owing to child-rearing breaks taken traditionally by women (even where parental leave is available to either sex)
◆ Access to learning opportunities, which are often made available through workplace education or employer sponsorship
◆ Undervaluing of the experience of women (which may have been gained outside the labour market or in part-time work)

compared with that of men (predominantly within the full-time labour market)

◆ Rigidity in labour market demands which women find more difficult to meet

◆ Women are more likely to be perceived as unwilling to be mobile or flexible.

In a church-related conference, we ought also to acknowledge that not all offices and positions are open to both sexes and that, even where there is no formal restriction, it is the experience of some women that there is resistance to their appointment or to their functioning or to their 'promotion'.

Men too, alongside female participants in the labour market, have seen very considerable changes in the employment field.

The structure of the economy has changed significantly the occupational balance within society, particularly away from heavy manufacturing industries towards light manufacturing and service industries. Some of this has been characterised as a 'feminisation' of the economy and, despite opportunities for guidance and counselling and for re-training, some men have found difficulty in finding employment in the newly developing sectors where the skills required and the dominant culture have seemed distant and alien to some male unemployed, leading to long-term unemployment and to alienation from the labour market. There has been particular growth in certain sectors of the skilled economy which some sections of the community have found it difficult to penetrate. The existence of a section of our society which is effectively excluded from economic participation continues to be a significant issue for our society.

The shift in employment patterns has not only been one of occupational structure. There have been generated a great many jobs that are part-time and/or temporary. Short or fixed term contract work has become more common. The impact of such developments is wide-ranging. Women in particular have found themselves in temporary and part-time jobs.[16] Job insecurity has motivated people to become dual income families in order to ensure continuity of income in case of redundancy or unemployment and has perhaps contributed to the need to be seen to work harder (an issue we shall consider further below).

The 'work harder' culture is attributable to other causes also. In very many companies and institutions, there has been a significant (sometimes swift, sometimes gradual) reduction in the size of the workforce. It is a common experience in both private and public sectors for employees to be covering the workload of a number of 'redundant' posts on a permanent basis. Downsizing has not been (and often is not intended to be) matched by a reduction in the total workload.

Flattening of structures may sometimes have resulted in a reduction of 'over-management' and have made organisations more efficient and cost-effective, but there have been negative effects also – eg levels of support and direction have been reduced, placing greater responsibility on more junior employees; promotional opportunities have been significantly reduced, with consequences for turnover in experienced staff and lack of motivation amongst those who might have reasonably expected promotion in a more extended structure. However superficially attractive such flattening exercises may be in accountancy terms, there are often human resource implications in terms of motivation and morale, support and management, stress and turnover.

Even such apparently positive developments as the empowerment of staff (either individually or in teams) can have negative outcomes if the structure does not support this development, leaving employees feeling overburdened with responsibility, unsupported by superiors, exploited and insecure (particularly if the empowerment is accompanied by a blame culture).

Technological advances, particularly in information technology, have had their impact on occupational structures and on the skills demand of companies. ICT has been amongst the most significant growth areas for employment, though also it has facilitated redundancies through 'efficiency savings'. In human resource terms, the introduction of information technology can have positive benefits, particularly in creating greater flexibility, in saving time on certain kinds of tasks and in reducing the need for travel. On the other hand, it affords an increased scope for intrusion into family life and private time (particularly amongst home-based workers), may put harsher deadline pressures on staff and can present human rights issues.

So, let me summarise the key elements:

◆ Women's participation in the labour market has increased significantly, but equality in pay and access to employment in certain occupational areas, in the more permanent and full-time sectors and at higher levels remains partly unachieved. A range of strategies to address direct and indirect discrimination, to combat cultural factors and to make necessary ancillary provision are required to meet this inequality across a number of fronts, extending beyond narrowly defined labour market issues.

◆ The labour market offers fewer opportunities for secure long-term full-time employment and women and unskilled men have in general less access to these jobs.

◆ The existence of a hard core of long term or never employed men continues to create and maintain a section of the community who feel themselves to have no significant stake socially and economically.

◆ Many of those in employment feel themselves to be under (and often objectively are under) pressure to take on more work and greater responsibility and to do so without the levels of support that they had formerly. Organisational restructuring and technological development have contributed to this. There is also (and this is to some extent a distinct issue from workload) a growing culture to engage in longer working hours.

WORK AND BEYOND WORK

Traditionally, the demands of work and family were managed by a segmentation – men went 'out to work' and women 'stayed at home', taking responsibilities respectively for the economic and domestic needs of the family. There was a division of labour between the 'provider' (male) and the 'carer' (female). In the middle of the last century, the distortion of this allocation of roles in time of war was thought to be an aberration which would be righted as part of a normalisation of life. 'One of the happiest innovations is the emergence of the housewife as a separate and honoured category of the population. In wartime no one disputed the complete partnership of women in communal life and there is unstinted appreciation of her contribution to war industry. But rearing babies through happy healthy childhood to independent maturity is even more important than wiring aeroplanes and is a very much more absorbing and exacting task'[17]. It is surely right that the nurture of children and the making of home should be regarded as valuable and necessary (Ps. 128). For increasing numbers of women, however, the issue has not been family or work, but an intention to combine the two spheres of life. 'For decades now women have been calling for a better work-life balance to help them to be productive workers and good mothers that they want to be.[18]

The increased participation in the labour market of women with children has brought the issues of tension between the demands of work and home and the need for balance to the fore as a social concern. While it remains true, as we have suggested above, that women bear the main burden of responsibility for both child and elder care, then there will continue to be clearly a specific gender dimension to the call for an improved balance. It is not a marginal issue: 78% of women with children between 6 and 13 years undertake paid work and 22% of workers expect to have elder care responsibilities within five years[6].

Two-thirds of women are reckoned to return to work within the first year of their child's birth[19]. The typical woman in the workforce is not one who has never or no longer has childcare responsibilities. For most then, there is the double burden of duties and the task of balancing loyalties and responsibilities.

How different is it for men? Men commonly identify their status as 'breadwinner' as one that carries satisfaction[20] and is understood by them as being expected of them (though in fact the expectation of fathers by women rates 'involvement' above the importance of the man as economic provider). Men most commonly describe 'financial necessity' as the main reason for their working; whereas just less than half of the female respondents in a survey cited 'financial necessity' and an equal number 'independence'.[21] As we have argued earlier, the existence of two incomes is often regarded as a bulwark against the risk of unemployment affecting one partner. And increasing consumerism places considerable pressures on parents to meet the demands of their children to keep up with their peers, a pressure that does not vary particularly in relation to family income.[22] The incidence of the dual income family is likely to remain a feature of our society. While the income of women from work often now forms an ongoing part of the family resources, this is more typically regarded as a 'contribution' and does not alter the relative status of the male and female earner. (The concept of 'pin money' as a description of female earnings is an enduring one!) But perhaps it remains true that male self-esteem is still more caught up with being the breadwinner, the economic provider. (Long term unemployed men with working partners can find this – as they may imagine it – rôle reversal as a threat to their sense of selfhood as a man and do not easily draw on alternative sources of self-esteem and identity.)

While there is little evidence of a lessening of male self-image as the main economic provider, there is more evidence of a shift towards an acknowledgement by husbands/ partners and fathers of other rôles as being of significance. For this, of course, there is pressure within the family. Working wives/female partners legitimately have an expectation that there should be a greater sharing in the domestic responsibilities, in particular in child-rearing (though this expectation is not so commonly translated into a reality by men at home[9,11]). Participation and partnership are sought, if not always delivered. The need for the father to show emotional commitment to family members and to provide a rôle model for their sons is increasingly impressed upon men. There is perhaps also paternal recognition that there are rewards to be had from involvement in family life. 'Now fathers too are calling for a fairer deal'.[18]

So, the demand and search for an improved work-life[23] balance may arise particularly from the increased incidence of women with children in the labour market and it is still true that women bear disproportionately the burden of dual responsibilities, but nonetheless it is not exclusively a 'women's issue'. For example, in a survey of two parent working families, respondents of both sexes indicated that, next to a pay rise, the change they would most welcome would be training for their supervisors in taking a more accommodating view when family crises arose.[24]

Where the work-life balance is out of equilibrium, the consequences for the employee and her/his family may include

- ◆ Recognition of resentment through not spending enough time with partner/ children
- ◆ Conflict with family members over lack of support
- ◆ Feelings of guilt
- ◆ Tensions between the demands of the different rôles
- ◆ Exhaustion
- ◆ Missing out on the social aspect of family life
- ◆ Handling of emergency situations, eg child illness
- ◆ The perceived call to perfection and an inability to live with 'good enough'
- ◆ The crossing of boundaries when there are difficulties (work 'intrudes' into family time/space and vice versa).

This is not a marginal concern of a small number of employees. One company[25] found that almost 70% of all employees thought that their work/family challenges would increase over the next five years.

A level of conflict between work and home is quite common and it quite often has significant impact on the person and their relationships. A selection of statistics from one survey may indicate something of the extent of the degree of conflict.[26] 43.7% of respondents said that occasionally (32.7% fairly frequently) 'worry or concern over my work interferes with my non-work activities and interests'. 35.8% indicated that occasionally (28% fairly frequently) 'other people in my life complain about how much time I have to spend on my job'. Again, 35.8% replied that occasionally (33.5% fairly frequently) 'things I want to do outside of my work can't get done because of the demands my job puts on my time'. These figures would seem to point to a significant measure of tension between work obligations and other calls on time and energy.[27]

And it is not only the employee who suffers through an un-resolved or poorly resolved tension between work and home. The employee's partner and family are deprived of the benefits of his/her significant involvement and may have to endure negative behaviour.

For the employer, there are a significant number of potential benefits in adopting and implementing policies that encourage a healthy work-life balance.

◆ Reduction in absenteeism and late-coming as employees are less under stress and their family-related absences are an acknowledged and (to some extent) planned-for element in the organisation

◆ Improved retention rates as employees do not have either to seek a more family-friendly employer or to change to employment whose pattern allows a better work-home balance

◆ Extended recruitment as applicants who would otherwise find the arrangements a deterrent to seeking employment with the organisation

◆ Greater diversity of employees as fewer categories of people are excluded from participation

◆ Improved performance as there is less conflict (internal to the employee and interpersonal) to interfere with work

◆ Broader perspective on issues as employees and the employer are encouraged to see the employees' 'external' world, not as something that is alien and hidden, but as something that enriches their involvement in the work organisation.

◆ Higher job satisfaction, as work is not seen to be a threat and a problem

◆ Higher commitment to the work organisation which is seen to be working in tune with, rather than against, the employee as a person.

There are potentially positive outcomes too for wider society which otherwise has to bear the consequences (socially and economically) of weaknesses and breakdown in adult relationships and in the upbringing of children.

The time is surely over when people define themselves primarily in terms of their employment (though in this country we still have a resilient but unhealthy pre-occupation with classifying people according to their paid work). We are increasingly recognising that, while we expect satisfaction through our working, there is life beyond work. We are shifting our priorities away from the assumption that work comes first and everything else is lower down. We are acknowledging the huge cost, humanly as well as economically, of allowing work to damage one of the core structures of our society, our families.[28]

We have to recognise too that life is not lived just in the two sectors of 'work' and 'home'. There is also 'community' and there requires to be space in people's lives (not merely time) to participate in the life of their community – in political life, in voluntary work, in social networks, in recreational pastimes. There are worrying signs of decline in sense of citizenship (eg numbers voting in elections, participation in community councils, membership of political parties) and, though many factors may influence this, it may be that there is increasingly a 'squeeze' which pushes out anything that lies beyond the two dominant areas of work and family. 'All work and no play' makes Jack and Jill very dull people indeed – and that does not enhance their involvement in work or family life.

What needs to happen then, if there is to be a more sustainable and healthy balance between work and family?

- ◆ We need to recognise that it is no longer relevant to organise work around a model that is based upon the assumption of the norm of a male employee with a female partner whose full-time responsibility is the care of the home and the children. We need to revise our assumptions about the nature of the labour market and of society. In particular, the growing place of women in employment and the need to share family commitments has to be taken much more seriously.

- ◆ We need a different ethic of work, leaving behind beliefs that work is intrinsically more important than home, that people are not working hard enough if they have space for family or personal life, that the balance between work and home has to be a battleground for the loyalty of the employee/ parent-partner. There is sometimes apparent a macho virility test that regards tensions and conflicts between family and work as a measure of employee commitment to company.

- ◆ We need a different values system that places people before production and profit and does not regard sacrifice as good in itself.

- ◆ We need a holistic perspective on human beings that does not compartmentalise their rôles but recognises the interconnectedness of the different 'parts' of their lives.

- ◆ We have to acknowledge that increasingly people do not put all their self-esteem and life-satisfaction eggs in the work basket. They have expectations that life rewards are to be and sometimes can only be found in other contexts. People do not look to work to meet all their human needs.

- ◆ We need to recognise that the culture of work organisations can be hostile to family demands and needs. This may be overt or implicit. It may be apparent in the organisation's indifference to the life of the employee outside of the company – what has been called 'the myth of separate worlds'. It assumes a clear distinction between those who are company-oriented and those who put their families first. It operationally acts to assert the predominance of the workplace. It values the company-first employee over those who seek to achieve a more equal balance and bases promotion and rewards on this. It functions more rigidly than flexibly. It assumes that child-care is primarily/wholly a women's rather than a parents' issue.

◆ We need to see that a good work-life balance can be a win-win situation for employing organisation and employee/family.

◆ We need to adopt organisational practices and processes[29] that are flexible and open and family-sensitive and to ensure that managers, supervisors and colleagues are aware of them, committed to them and able to implement them.

TIME

Home-work balance has both quantitative and qualitative aspects. Qualitatively, it is concerned about the extent to which people are able to involve themselves meaningfully and significantly in relationships and responsibilities beyond the work sphere. Quantitatively, it is about the amount of time being spent at work.

While there is now greater diversity in working patterns, the typical is still 35-40 hours or longer, with women tending to work shorter hours and men longer. Parents at Work research[26] reported that of respondents:

64% routinely worked beyond their contractual hours
55% believed this to be the accepted workplace culture
35% did so under direct management pressure and
20% did so out of fear of job loss.

In another study on the reasons for long work hours[30], the participants indicated that the main causes were:

heavy workload 36%
not letting colleagues or clients down 19%
love of job 16%.

Research conducted for the Department of Education and Employment[31] concluded that

1 in 9 employees worked more than 60 hours per week

1 in 8 employees still worked weekends

80% of workplaces had workers doing more than their standard hours

25% of entitled female employees took less than 18 weeks maternity leave.

Downsizing changes in staffing numbers very often have not been matched by reduction in overall workload within the organisation and it is commonly reported that 'redundancies' have not meant that the job is no longer required, but that the organisation wishes to make a saving while spreading the duties across remaining employees. (This of course has implications not only quantitatively on workload but also qualitatively in the challenge/stress that may be involved in taking on unfamiliar duties.)

The UK has become one of the nations with the longest working hours. For example, in relation to workers in manufacturing industries, as of 1998[32]:

Country	Working hours
Japan	1947
USA	1991
West Germany (then)	1517
France	1672
UK	1925.

A BBC poll published in September 1999 indicated that one in five workers was being forced to sign opt-outs from the EU working hours directive introduced in October 1998.[33]

Those men with greatest family responsibilities were amongst those who undertook the longest working hours.[21] Men with young children (because of the financial demands upon their earning power?) are far more likely (four-times) than the average employee to exceed their contractual minimum hours. Lone parent fathers are reported to work an average of 55 hours per week. Clearly, there is a tension between the economic demands on fathers and the social demands.

How welcome is this trend? A survey for the European Foundation for Living and Working Conditions[34] showed evidence of a widespread wish for shorter working hours. Only 35% of the respondents who were presently employed were happy with their working hours: 11% wanted to work more but 54% less. Indeed 42% of those in employment wanted to reduce their working hours by 5 hours or more.

One must presume that the justification for long working hours must lie in assumptions about a positive correlation between hours input and the productivity output, but this is a very questionable belief. When workers with working weeks longer than 48 hours were questioned[30], 73% admitted making more mistakes, only 29% believed that those who work long hours were more productive and 36% spent significant amounts of time re-doing work or solving problems arising from disorganised or inefficient organisation. Of course, with certain occupational groups, there are health and safety issues involved in worker error, for themselves, for colleagues and for clients. Our cognitive and motor performance is impaired by working without appropriate sleeping time to an extent that can be compared with functioning after the intake of significant amounts of alcohol.[35] Professor Carey Cooper[36] has argued, 'We have to understand that long hours do not mean workers are more productive. If you work an extra two or three hours per week there is probably no increased productivity'. It cannot be assumed too that all the time that employees spend *at* work is spent *in* work. There is a form of presenteeism in which the worker is physically on site but not undertaking work-related duties.

There may also be negative effects upon the company in terms of its ability to attract and retain employees, especially those who have choice.

Long hours too may be a symptom of other problems within the organisation: eg an inability to organise work efficiently and effectively; a failure to delegate responsibility; a lack of trust within the organisation; an inappropriate allocation of responsibilities across the organisation leaving some over- and some under-employed; a failure to train workers forcing them to time-greedy trial and error approaches to solving problems.

If, then, there is little evidence of the usefulness of long working hours and perhaps even a suspicion that they may point to organisational weaknesses, what encourages a perpetuation of this practice?

◆ In an insecure labour market, employees are readily motivated by fear that if they are not seen to work as hard as colleagues, they will be thought to be less productive and less committed to the organisation and may therefore be more vulnerable to redundancy measures or to being passed over for promotion

◆ A distorted work ethic valuing 'hard work' interprets this quantitatively rather than qualitatively, focusing then on how long one works rather than what one does and achieves

◆ The culture of many organisations remains, despite the presence of more women, a 'macho' culture in which strength is demonstrated by the ability to endure oppressive working hours

◆ Information and communication technology innovations have put additional pressure on employees to respond on short timescales

◆ Commitment to client can bring a self-imposed pressure to maintain levels of service and productivity even in the face of severe reduction in staffing resources

- ◆ The development of work obsession[37](workaholism) leading to disturbed relaxation ability which can seem to the employee to be satisfactory, but in the longer term has negative social and health consequences
- ◆ Work overload is being disguised through long working hours, which may be effective in the short term but is likely to be more problematic in the longer term[38].

But if such long working hours are not demonstrably good for the employing organisation, they are clearly not good for the employee and her/his dependents. Again, we may cite Professor Carey who asserts that there is 'a clear relationship between ill health and consistently working long hours'. For many years, for example, there has been a recognised link between long working hours and coronary heart disease. In two such studies, individuals under 45 working 48+ hours pw were found to be twice at risk of death from heart attack compared with those who worked less than 40 hours pw[39]; one in four young coronary patients were found to be working in two jobs and two in five had been working more than 60 hours pw[40]. Other related health problems reported and believed to be related to extended working days include back problems, stress symptoms, insomnia and increased fatigue.[41]

And we ought not to assume that the absence of physical health problems means that all is well. Without seeking to be prescriptive as to what constitutes a 'good life', we may want to argue that a life in which there is no time for recreation, for non-work relationships, for being rather than doing, falls short of the ideal.

These long hours impact on others too[30]. 30% of such employees acknowledged that the hours they work puts strain on their relationship with their partner and 13% indicated that it had led to break-up with a partner or boy/girlfriend. 44% of those who worked long hours and had small school children reported that they felt that their hours caused damage to their relationship with their children. More than two out of five acknowledged that they had missed one of their children's birthday celebrations or a school event in the previous year. Extended hours are likely also to increase the probability of the swing-door effect, where life partners spend little time with each other or with their dependents.

As we noted earlier too, an over-strong focus on work has implications for voluntary and community involvement.

- ◆ While occasional long hours are not in themselves harmful, as a way of life they can inflict harm on health, family life and community participation.
- ◆ The alleged benefits of long hours to employing organisations

must be questioned. Extended working may be a symptom of organisational sickness rather than a positive good.

◆ Organisations need to challenge their internal culture where this encourages over-extended working hours and to address those organisational issues which contribute to such a culture.

THE WORKPLACE

In the two previous sections, we have been concerned with the extent to which work may take an over-exaggerated place in life, either in its percentage of time or in its importance.

We turn now to issues of quality within the work sphere itself. This is, of course, a vast area and we can no more than touch upon a number of aspects.

Work not only takes up a major part of our time, it is also a significant source of stress.[42]

Sources of stress:

◆ Insecurity arising from downsizing, out-sourcing and sub-contracting

◆ Workload – both in quantity and timescale

◆ Poor interpersonal relationships with colleagues, managers and supervisors, including poor communication, social isolation, interpersonal conflict

◆ Difficulty in coping with demands, which may have been caused by changes in rôle and responsibilities or by lack of training/induction to meet change or by inappropriate promotion or by inability to influence scheduling

◆ Perceived lack of personal control – typically, the less control, the more severe a problem tends to be regarded

◆ Lack of coping strategies or organisational practices which inhibit their use

◆ Career development issues – over or under promotion, stagnation, lack of status and respect

◆ Even positive changes which are intended to enhance the work environment may produce stress,[43] eg flexible or home working may allow freedom or be more compatible with other responsibilities, but it may result in the employee overworking and never feeling off-duty

◆ Poor fit between the person and their situation – either the employee's aptitudes and attitudes do not match the requirements of the organisation, or the job environment does not meet the worker's needs[44]

◆ Lack of support, particularly from people in charge
◆ Rôle ambiguity and rôle conflict
◆ Organisational change, particularly when this is constant or unsupported or unclear or non-participative
◆ Lack of definition of organisational objectives and priorities
◆ Low job satisfaction, including under-utilisation of knowledge and skills, lack of task variety
◆ Insufficiency of resources to achieve work goals
◆ Lack of feedback on performance.

Studies tend to concentrate upon acute events which occasion stress and there is relatively poorer acknowledgement of chronic conditions which are stressors.

Even our human capacity for adaptation/coping in the short term may have longer term negative consequences – 'the diseases of adaptation'[45]. Of course, stress is not always intolerable and will not necessarily result in psychological or physiological ill-health or other than short-term damage. Some stress is within our normal coping ability, our homeostatic limits, and may even be regarded as a stimulus.

Nonetheless, there are significant reasons why employers should have strategies for stress-related issues. Absenteeism through stress-induced health problems costs UK industry in the region of 40 million working days each year.[46] While figures rely on self-report and therefore unreliability may be an issue, there is evidence[47] that up to 60% of work absence may be due to stress-related disorders.

Organisational strategies to deal with stress issues may focus on

◆ the individual and/or
◆ the organisation
◆ and may be aimed at
◆ prevention
◆ recognition and response
◆ rehabilitation.

The employee-focused approaches (usually personal stress management programmes) might at first sight seem to be most concerned with the individual's needs, but their weakness lies in the extent to which they may ignore chronic organisational issues which underlie the particular problem and do not acknowledge the interaction between the person and their environment. The model is medical in character, 'curing' the employee of his or her problem. It has a tendency to be self-contained, unrelated to the diagnosis and remedying of the underlying causes. Of the individual and the environment, the latter may be the more 'sick' of the two. One can see the short term advantages of this approach, mainly that it is minimally disruptive to the organisation as a whole. They may also be attractive to the individual concerned as they seem to be a practical and immediate answer and sometimes affected individuals have a low awareness of the broader strategic problems. (For example, A's problem with his/her manager may reflect a lack of management training or a communication problem or an absence of effective supervision of managers.) This criticism is not to suggest that relaxation techniques, assertiveness training and personal coping mechanisms are not beneficial (though the evidence for this in the long term is perhaps weak). Our contention, however, is that by themselves they can ignore the more fundamental causes of stress and unhappiness within an organisation. As one team of researchers concluded[48]: 'job redesign and organisational change remain the preferred approaches to stress management because they focus on reducing or eliminating the sources of the problem in the work environment'. Where individuals are the focus, their circumstances and needs become problematised. The issue of childcare, say, is often regarded simply as an individual problem and treated only as a women's issue, whereas the question of care facilities, or flexible working provision, or changing the organisational culture is a wider one. To address only the individual's needs in isolation can become arbitrary, is often looked on as 'doing the employee a favour' and does nothing to alter the prevailing organisational culture.

◆ Stress is a major issue within employing institutions and it has consequences not simply for the individuals concerned but for the whole organisation and for the economy.
◆ Stress management programmes and the like require to be complemented by the identification and solving of wider organisational issues, including the changing of organisational culture, structures and processes.

CONCLUSION

This article has been an attempt to look at the world of work with a view to seeing how it might be more human-friendly. We have been able to review only a small corner of the employment field, issues of work-life balance, working hours and stress at work. We are conscious that there are many still outside the labour market or marginalized within it. We acknowledge that, in a globalised marketplace, there are justice and equality and human rights issues in which our economy is implicated. Our focus has been a narrow one, perhaps too narrow a one, but that is not to suggest that its issues are unimportant. Work remains a fundamental part of the lives of many of us. It affirms or denies our humanity.

A CHRISTIAN CODA

One cannot address this article to a church-sponsored assembly without taking seriously the call 'Physician, heal thyself' (Luke 4:23). We are ever at risk of lecturing the world, drawing attention to the motes in its eye, while ignoring the plank in our own. (Matt 7:3; Luke 6:41) Therefore, let us acknowledge our own areas of weakness (or at least some of them).

- ◆ To what extent are offices within the church open to all on an equality of access basis? Where these are restricted, does the theological or traditional rationale outweigh considerations of justice and equality? Where there is theoretically open access to offices, does there nonetheless remain direct and indirect discrimination on gender or other grounds?
- ◆ Do we value the work of all within the church equally or is the work of some (and, in particular, paid work) seen to be more worthy of status and dignity? Is higher regard afforded to stipendiary offices than to 'voluntary' offices?
- ◆ Do we ensure that those in ecclesiastical vocations are encouraged to maintain a healthy balance between their 'work' and other aspects of life? And do the attitudes of congregations etc support or work against this position?
- ◆ How 'male' is the culture and ethos and networking of the church?
- ◆ How greedy is the church in its consumption of people's time and energy? Does it eat up resources that might more appropriately be for family or other community purposes?
- ◆ Do we have a holistic view of our church workers? And of their needs? Or are we interested in them primarily/solely in their church rôle?
- ◆ Have our strategies to cope with downsizing in ministry resources recognised the additional pressures that they put on clergy and others?
- ◆ Do we take sufficient steps to ensure that church workers do not regularly engage in unhealthy working hours? Or do we regard constant availability and long hours as signs of true commitment?
- ◆ Do we regard stress amongst church workers as being rooted in themselves or do we acknowledge the organisational factors that contribute to stress? Do we have systematic review processes

which not only evaluate performance but identify support needs? Do we have processes which not only support clergy and other church workers in stress but appraise and address the organisational factors involved?

◆ In relation to church workers, do we take seriously human needs for job satisfaction, growth and development, sense of personal control, clarity of rôle and congruity of values, support in coping with change and with challenges, clarity of direction and adequate resourcing, consistent feedback and reward?

◆ How do we handle issues of misfit between person and environment? Are our models disciplinary in character? Do we face up to the existence of this problem?

CHAPTER FIVE

BREAKING THROUGH TO A FRESH APPROACH TO SPIRITUALITY

Gerard W. Hughes

TODAY, CHURCHES EMPTYING, SPIRITUALITY MORE POPULAR – WHY?

In Britain today an increasing number of people are estranged from Christian institutions. Church attendance in Britain fell by over 20% in the ten years from 1989 – 1998. In 1987 Gordon Heald, then director of Gallup Poll in Britain, and Dr David Hay, of Nottingham University, undertook a survey which showed that 48% of the adult population in Britain claimed to have had some spiritual experience in their lives which was still affecting them. Thirteen years later, in another survey which they undertook together with the BBC's recent 'Soul of Britain' series, the results suggest that more than 76% of the national population admit to having had a spiritual or religious experience. These are astonishing statistics which present the Churches with a daunting challenge. To whom are the Churches meant to minister? To all human beings, or only to churchgoing members of their own Christian denomination? To what percentage of the population do they, in fact, minister? Probably to less than 8%. What is the average age of those to whom they minister? I have no statistical answer, but from my experience of church services and church meetings, the average age of regular churchgoers is probably about 55 years, and rising annually.

It is said that when the Aborigines first saw Captain Cook's ship approach the Australian coast, they took no notice and continued with their fishing, but when the long boats were let down from the ship, they at once took evasive action. The Aborigines' minds could not apprehend the large ship, but they could cope with rowing boats. Are these astonishing statistics too momentous and threatening for the Churches to grasp, leading us to focus our attention on matters of church maintenance, with which we are more familiar? The first question which all the Churches in Scotland must face is, 'Why is the Good News, which we are to preach to the whole world, failing to hold even the committed members of our own congregations?'

I have spent hours talking with people who are disillusioned and disaffected from their church. Very often it is the most Christ-centred and committed who are the most critical, and their criticism, although it is directed against what they call 'The Church', is usually criticism of their clergy. The criticism becomes boring in its repetitiveness: the Church is hypocritical, out of touch, more interested in its own structures than in the lives of its members, the clergy are unwilling to listen, lack compassion, conviction.

I write this as a member of the clergy. I know how unjust these criticisms can be when fired indiscriminately at every cleric of every denomination, but what we must not do is seize upon the unfairness of some of the criticism and use it as an excuse for refusing to listen to any of it. Unless we face the questions honestly, there can be no change. The questions will not disappear because church authorities are angered by them. If the decrease in church membership continues at the present rate, our churches will be empty by 2050!

THE SPLIT NATURE OF OUR SPIRITUALITY

One reason for the failure of the Churches to communicate the Good News is the split nature of the spirituality which the Churches present. By 'split nature' I mean the way in which God is presented as split off from ordinary everyday life. This split runs very deep. It is so deep, and we are so used to it, that we can fail to notice it. People outside of the established churches are searching for a spirituality which is less split and more 'holistic', meaning a spirituality which takes account of body, mind and spirit.

The latest edition of the Concise Oxford Dictionary gives under SPIRITUALITY: 1. 'Concerning the spirit as opposed to matter. 2. concerned with sacred or religious things; holy; divine; inspired. 3 (of the mind etc.) refined, sensitive; not concerned with the material. 4 (of a relationship etc.) concerned with the soul; or spirit etc., not with external reality.' This definition clearly distinguishes the material from the spiritual, the sacred from the profane, the soul from the body, and raises some interesting questions for all of us. What kind of person would I be if I were to become spiritual according to this definition, giving all my attention to spiritual things as distinct from material. What kind of home would I have and what kind of friends, if any? If I were to go on a long distance flight and were to pray to God for protection, what kind of pilot would I pray for? A pilot who was spiritual according to the dictionary definition, whose attention was totally on the spirit, not on external reality, or would I prefer a good reliable atheist whose primary interest was in bringing this material plane and its material contents safely back to earth?

Our religious vocabulary reflects this split. We distinguish spirit from matter, the natural from the supernatural, the sacred from the profane, the temporal from the eternal, the soul from the body, faith from reason. These are necessary and useful distinctions, but they are commonly understood in ways which are neither necessary, nor useful. We understand the distinctions as though they applied to different layers of reality, as though the supernatural hovers above and is vastly superior to the natural, as though matter was a stuff of no real importance, while spirit was of supreme importance, as though the sacred was the place where God is, and the secular or profane was the place where God is not. This split spirituality has its advantages: it keeps God from interfering in our lives and plans. The more we emphasise the sacred, the spiritual, the eternal, the more free we can be to get on with our business affairs and dealings, convincing ourselves of God's support while remaining free from God's interference!

EXPLORING THE SPLIT

A way of exploring this split for oneself is through an imaginative exercise which can be repeated frequently, for each time it is done, it can offer new insights.

Imagine a ring at your doorbell one evening. On answering, you discover that the caller is the Risen Lord himself. Somehow you know, beyond any shadow of doubt, that it is he. What do you do now? Do not try to work out elaborate answers to this question: just imagine the scene, and see what imagination offers.

Presumably you invite Jesus in. In the course of the evening you may find yourself making fatuous statements to Jesus, Lord of all creation, like, 'Do make yourself at home'. Jesus gratefully accepts your invitation. Now take a leap in your imagination of two weeks. Jesus is still at home: what is it like at home now? To assist your imagination you might recall some of Jesus' statements recorded in the Gospels, things you wish he had never said, like 'Do you suppose that I am here to bring peace on earth? No, I tell you, but rather division. For from now on a household of five will be divided: three against two and two against three; the father divided against the son, the son against father, mother against daughter, daughter against mother, mother-in-law against daughter-in-law, daughter-in-law against mother-in-law.' (Lk. 12: 51-53). So what has Jesus said or done in the last two weeks which might have caused dissension in the family?

Having invited Jesus to be at home, he has now begun inviting his friends to your house. Who were his friends in the Gospels, and what did respectable people say about his friends? What kind of people are coming along your road now, and what is happening to local property values?

Jesus' stay is bringing you trouble at home and trouble with the neighbours. You are no longer so anxious as before to keep Jesus all to yourself, so you have him invited to your local church to give a talk. You remember the talk he once gave to the chief priests, the scribes and the Pharisees, all of them most religious men, in the course of which he assured them that the prostitutes and the tax gatherers would enter the kingdom of God before they did. He gives substantially the same address at your local parish church and there is uproar, the parish losing some of its wealthiest and most important members.

You return home with Jesus. You are now in trouble at home, in trouble with your neighbours, in trouble with the Church. You cannot expel Jesus, for he is Lord of all creation. A possible solution might be to examine your house carefully, find a suitable cupboard, clear it out, clean and decorate it, sparing no expense. Have good strong locks fitted to the door, invite Jesus to step inside, lock the door, place a lamp and flowers in front, and each time you go past, you bow deeply and reverently. You now have Jesus in your house, but he does not interfere any more.

KEEPING GOD REVERENTLY OUT OF THE WAY

In our preaching, teaching, pastoral work and worship, is this what we have done with God? We show great reverence, have magnificent churches, take great care over liturgy, sacred music, songs, give careful attention to our credal statements, our church discipline, but we also take remarkable care to ensure that God does not interfere with our ordinary, everday affairs, because God outside the cupboard can cause havoc in every aspect of our lives, as the imaginative story illustrates.

One illustration of our unwillingness to allow God to interfere with our everyday affairs is the common assumption that politics should be kept out of religion, a principle dear to the heart of every despot. Totalitarian regimes are often very supportive of religious movements, provided the adherents' spirituality is clearly split. Religious tolerance gives the regime the appearance of respectability: the split spirituality ensures that the religious movement remains harmless.

Scottish church leaders are to be congratulated on their clear public stand against Britain's possession, deployment or threatened use of nuclear weapons. ACTS is to be congratulated on its emphasis on social justice, peace and reconciliation, and on its interest in inter-faith work. However, for many years, among British Church leaders, with a very few exceptions, no clear voices were heard protesting against our possession of nuclear weapons. Still in Britain today, no political party dares to question our nuclear deterrence policy, and the vast majority of Christians still support it. This fact raises fundamental questions about the nature of our spirituality, of our understanding of God and of God's relationship to human life and to all creation.

Because our spirituality is split, we can pray solemnly for peace while at the same time proceeding to plan mass murder. The split runs deep and includes our tendency to divinise what we are pleased to call 'reason'. and to ignore feelings and emotion. As our relationship with God is a relationship of the whole person, a relationship of intimate love, our split spirituality stifles the very essence of our relationship with God. Here is an imaginative exercise to illustrate the way in which we normally prevent God from interfering with our practical living. Imagine that I am in favour of our nuclear deterrence policy and that I am invited to pray publicly for peace at a large Christian gathering. Instead of a vague prayer, 'Vouchsafe, O Lord, peace in our day ————'. I shall include in this prayer my thinking about peace. In reading it, notice what effect it has on your feelings. Our feelings and emotions are usually quicker and more intelligent than our conscious minds: they spot more quickly the creative and the destructive forces around us and within us. To ignore feelings is as sensible as advising someone to drive resolutely on our roadways but to ignore all road signs and traffic lights. One of the essential things in a new approach to spirituality is that we should learn a new respect for the wisdom of our feelings, become more aware of them, and learn to read them..

'Dear Lord, inspire our scientists that they may invent yet more lethal weaponry. Preserve us from any unfortunate accident in its testing, lest we suffer a worse disaster than Chernobyl. Bless our economy that we may put these weapons into plentiful production, otherwise they will not deter. Have a special care of the hungry and the homeless, the sick and the aged, both of our own and of other lands, until such time as our defence commitments allow us to contribute a little more to these worthy purposes, strengthen our leaders so that they remain resolute in carrying through a strong defence policy, Drive out from our midst any who, by thought, word or deed undermine our national security , and grant us the protection of nuclear weaponry now and forever. Amen.'

If this prayer arouses strong feelings within us, we need to acknowledge the feelings, not ignore them, and ask ourselves the reason for these felt reactions. Our feelings and emotions can be changed by drugs and diet, but normally our feelings arise out of desire. When our desires are satisfied, our mood is good and we can be all charm to those around us. When our desires are frustrated our mood is bad: we grind inside and take it out on others. What is the desire underlying my felt reactions? Is it desire for my kingdom, my security, my status, my way of life, or is it desire for God's kingdom of justice, peace, love for all peoples, for all creation?

THE SEARCH TODAY FOR A MORE HOLISTIC SPIRITUALITY

In Britain today, millions are in search of a spirituality which gives meaning to our lives, a spirituality which speaks to body, mind and spirit, not to spirit only. This is what New Age people are looking for, and that is why they show such interest in Celtic spirituality, an earthed spirituality, which finds God in everyday things. This search for a more 'holistic' spirituality is also to be found among committed churchgoers. The annual ecumenical magazine called 'Retreats', which advertises the programmes of retreat houses throughout Britain, makes fascinating reading. Thirty years ago, most retreat houses offered weekend retreats for lay people which consisted in a series of talks, given by the priest / minister, to which the lay people listened, then reflected and prayed on afterwards, the whole retreat usually conducted in silence. Today there are retreats described as 'Clay and Painting', 'Dance and Movement', 'Massage', 'Aroma Therapy'. 'Interpreting your Dreams', 'Healing Life's Hurts', 'Healing of Memories', 'The Enneagram', 'Myers-Briggs retreats' etc. While this is a promising development, and while Christian spirituality must include body, mind and spirit, not all 'holistic' spirituality is necessarily Christian. God told Israel, 'Be holy, as I the Lord your God am holy'. God did not say, 'Be holistic, as I, the Lord your God am holistic'!

THE DIFFERENCE BETWEEN BEING HOLY AND BEING HOLISTIC

To illustrate the truth that being holistic is not the same thing as being holy, ponder this example. Imagine two men: one is a very intuitive character, artistic, imaginative, a powerful orator, very influential. He is also very abstemious, a vegetarian, teetotal, non-smoking. The second is a bent-over man who suffers from arthritis, is of melancholic temperament and afflicted with suicidal tendencies. Which of the two is the more holistic? The first is obviously the more holistic: this is a thumbnail sketch of Adolf Hitler. The second is of the Abbé Huvelin, a famous French spiritual director, who died at the beginning of the twentieth century. He looked after Charles de Foucauld and the Baron von Hügel, among many others. Von Hügel wrote of his visits to the Abbé Huvelin, describing the effect this man, wracked with pain, had on him. Von Hügel always came away feeling peace and joy. This brings us to the heart of the matter – what is the meaning of holiness?

HOLINESS MEANS THE HOLY ONE DWELLS WITHIN US

In his letters, St Paul addresses the Corinthians as 'the saints', the holy ones. He then goes on to upbraid them for incest, fornication and taking each other to court, not the kind of behaviour expected of saints, of holy people. Paul calls them the holy ones because the Holy One, the Spirit of God, dwells within them. Spirituality is concerned with our becoming aware of this truth, the truth of every person, for in God all human beings 'live and move and have their being'.

We are all made in the image of God, but 'image' does not catch the intimacy of the relationship. Jesus said, 'I am the Vine, you are the branches' (Jn. 15:5), and he prayed 'May they all be one. Father, may they be one in us, as you are in me and I am in you——' (Jn. 17:21). St. Paul prays for the Ephesians, 'Out of his infinite glory, may he give you the power through his Spirit for your hidden self to grow strong, so that Christ may live in your hearts through faith'. (Eph. 3:16) Paul also writes, 'I live now not with my own life, but with the life of Christ who lives in me'. (Gal. 2:20) There is a homily from the early centuries of Christianity in which the anonymous author imagines Jesus descending to hell after his death and having a conversation with Adam. The conversation ends with Jesus saying, 'Adam, arise, come forth. Henceforth, you and I will be one undivided person'. The whole purpose and object of our lives as Christians is to be at one with Christ, the Holy One, our ultimate identity. A good exercise is to hear Jesus speak that phrase to you now. Hear it come out from the core of your being. Then try to respond and see what happens! The phrase starts to clash with our common sense, our layers of unbelief, our practical atheism. Stay with the phrase until it reduces you to stunned silence: then hear what your heart is saying!

THE HOLY ONE IS TRANSCENDENT - SIGNS OF TRANSCENDENCE IN US

What is this God like, in whom we live, who is our 'spirituality', the ultimate reference point of our whole being? God is both transcendent and immanent. In describing God as transcendent, we assert that God must always be for us mystery, always greater and beyond anything we can think or imagine, a God who cannot be defined, who can never adequately be known by any human mind, a God who can never be domesticated, despite all our attempts to do so. That is why the Church is called the 'Pilgrim Church', always on the way, like the Israelites wandering through the desert following the pillar of cloud, which was always ahead of them. The Church, if she is to be true to herself, must always be pointing beyond herself towards God. All her structures must always be pointing beyond herself: her liturgy, teachings, rules and regulations must never be considered ends in themselves, for so to consider them would be idolatry. The purpose of all church structures must be to enable us, both as individuals and as a Church, to become more perceptive and more responsive to the Spirit of God, the Holy One, dwelling within us and amongst us.

Because God dwells within us and God is our ultimate identity, there must be transcendent elements in us. There is not space to develop this truth in any detail here, but the fact that we can be aware of our own ignorance, of the limitations of our own minds, points to some kind of awareness greater than our consciousness. In all true faith in God there must be an element of agnosticism, an awareness of our not knowing. Fundamentalism, understood as the assertion that we know the ultimate truth about God and ourselves, diminishes both God and ourselves. Other signs in us of the transcendent include our ability to be wonderstruck, the nature of human desire, an insatiable hunger for we-know-not-what, our hunger for freedom and unwillingness to be totally subject to any human individual or group, any ideology or political system. The Church, therefore, must be society's question mark, always vigilant that society does not slide into political or religious idolatry. Belief in God, who is transcendent is the ultimate guarantee of our freedom, of our human rights and civil liberties.

To be holy will include awareness of our own ignorance and of the limitations of the human intellect, the ability to laugh at our own and other peoples' pomposity and pretentiousness. It will also include being a person of strong desire, being passionate, being a lover of freedom, an honest searcher, with an ability to be wonderstruck.

GOD IS ALSO IMMANENT. HOLINESS EXPRESSED IN COMPASSION

God is also immanent; that is, God is in all things, in all people, in all events and is, in St Augustine's words, 'Nearer to me than I am to myself'. Most of us can accept either that God is transcendent, or that God is immanent: what most of us find impossibly difficult is that God can be both transcendent and immanent at the same time! What is this God like, who is my ultimate identity, nearer to me than I am to myself?

The characteristic quality of Israel's God is God's compassion for all creation. It is this quality of compassion which explains the fearsome 'God of wrath' passages in the Hebrew prophets. The prophets keep reminding Israel that God has entered into a Covenant with them and they describe the Covenant in terms of a marriage:-

> For now your creator will be your husband,
> his name, Yahweh Sabaoth;
> Your redeemer will be the Holy One of Israel,
> he is called God of the whole earth. (Isaiah 54:5)

Because God has married Israel, Israel must now mirror in all her behaviour, whether towards other Israelites or to the stranger, the mercy and compassion of God.

> Yahweh spoke to Moses; he said;
> Be holy, for I, Yahweh your God, am holy. (Leviticus 19:2)

In chapter 19 of Leviticus, being holy includes not gathering the gleanings of the harvest, nor stripping your vines bare, in order to ensure that the poor and the stranger may have something to eat. Being holy prohibits every form of deceit and fraud, of injustice and vengeance, and demands that we love our neighbour as ourselves. Holiness is a very earthed quality, manifest most clearly in the way we relate to other people and to creation. The split nature of our spirituality has made us think of holiness as 'endowed or invested with extreme purity, or sublimity'! Because God is God of mercy and compassion, therefore the wrath of God is against his people when they exploit and oppress the poor and the powerless. Here are a few brief examples:-

GOD'S WRATH SPRINGS FROM GOD'S COMPASSION

The first is from Amos, the earliest recorded prophet. He was a poor man from the South, sent by God to preach to the affluent and sophisticated North. God filled him with zeal, but left him short on tact. Here is Amos addressing the fashionable ladies of Samaria:-

> Listen to this, you cows of Bashan
> living in the mountains of Samaria,
> oppressing the needy, crushing the poor,
> saying to your husbands, 'Bring us something to drink!'
> The Lord Yahweh swears this by his holiness;
> the days are coming to you now
> when you will be dragged out with hooks,
> the very last of you with prongs.
> Out you will go, each by the nearest breach in the wall,
> to be driven all the way to Hermon.
> It is Yahweh who speaks. (Amos 4:1-3)

GOD'S LOATHING OF DYSFUNCTIONAL LITURGY

The Samaritans, who oppress the needy and crush the poor, are keen on solemn liturgies. Amos addresses them on this subject:-

> I hate and despise your feasts,
> I take no pleasure in your solemn festivals . . .
> Let me have no more of the din of your chanting,
> no more of your strumming on harps.
> But let justice flow like water,
> and integrity lie an unfailing stream. (Amos 5:21-24)

This theme runs through all the prophets. Solemn liturgies and external acts of devotion are abhorrent to God if they are not the expression of genuine compassion for the suffering of others.

> When you stretch out your hands
> I turn my eyes away.
> You may multiply your prayers,
> I shall not listen.
> Your hands are covered with blood.
> wash, make yourselves clean.
> Take your wrongdoing out of my sight. (Isaiah 1:15-16)

HOLINESS TO BE EXPRESSED IN SOCIAL JUSTICE

The God of the Hebrew prophets is God of the now, screaming at us for the blatant injustice of World debt, for the exploitation of the Third World by the First, for our iniquitous economy, which constantly enriches the few at the cost of the many, widens the gap between rich and poor countries, rich and poor individuals, ravages the earth's resources and jeopardises the survival of future generations for the sake of short term profits. The prophetic message is always addressed to nations, never to individuals, except in so far as an individual represents a nation. We cannot claim to be Christian if, at the same time and for whatever excuse, we are refusing to look at our own nation, its social and political structures, our relationships with one another within the nation, but also our relationships with other nations, which includes our trade regulations, immigration policies, defence policy, arms trade, the nature of our overseas aid. We cannot ignore these questions, or declare them to be no concern of religious people. As far as the God of Abraham, Isaac and Jacob, the God of Our Lord Jesus Christ is concerned, to ignore these questions is to be guilty of practical atheism. Scotland is blessed in the work and influence of the Iona community with its message of justice and peace, with its emphasis on the universality of Christ's call. Interest in justice and peace issues is not an optional extra for the more socially minded Christians of left-wing tendency: it is integral to all true Christian faith, a truth which is constantly emphasised in the work of ACTS.

HOLINESS IN JESUS' LIFE, TEACHING AND PASSION

In Jesus, image of the unseen God, the compassion of God is manifest. His compassion is the expression of his holiness, a holiness to which every Christian is called. Jesus' life is characterised by his relationship with God, whom he addresses as 'Abba', a child's name for father. Therefore, in our spirituality, familiarity with 'Abba', God of compassion for all peoples, is of primary importance. This familiarity is nurtured through the practice of private prayer. Jesus first recorded words in the Gospel are addressed to his parents after they found him in the Temple, 'Did you not know that I must be about my father's business?' His last words on the cross are, 'Into thy hands I commend my spirit'. In describing his public life, the Gospels have a constant refrain, 'He took pity on them and healed their sick'. Jesus' God is a God of compassion, as his life and all his teachings testify.

God is the father of the prodigal son, a God who is presented as spending his days waiting for the return of his son. 'While he was still a long way off, his father saw him and was moved with pity'. He is a father without dignity, for he runs out to meet him 'He ran to the boy, clasped him in his arms and kissed him tenderly'. When the boy confesses 'I have sinned against heaven and against you. I no longer deserve to be called your son.' the father does not appear to listen. He turns to the servants and says, 'Quick, bring out the best robe and put it on him; put a ring on his finger and sandals on his feet. Bring the calf we have been fattening and kill it; we are going to have a feast' (Luke 15:22-23), words which reflect a wonderful description of God in the book of Wisdom, translated in the Authorised version as, 'He winketh at our transgressions that we may amend'! (Wisdom 11:23)

In the parable of the Wedding Feast, God is presented as the King whose one anxiety is that all places should be filled at his son's wedding feast. When some invited guests refuse the invitation, the king tells his servants to go out into the highways and bring everyone in, the halt, the lame and the blind. The servants return and report to the king that they have brought everyone in, 'wicked and good alike'! (Matthew 22:10) This is disgraceful behaviour on God's part, behaviour which Christian churches have, on the whole, taken care not to follow! The parable of the lost sheep, the lost drachma, the parable of Dives and Lazarus, all of them emphasise the compassion of God. In Jesus' description of our Final Judgement, the questions asked will not be to which Church, if any, we belonged, the creeds we affirmed, the religious services attended, observances fulfilled: the one question will be about our compassion. 'I was hungry', 'I was thirsty', 'I tell you solemnly, in so far as you neglected to do this to one of the least of these, you neglected to do it to me'. (Matthew 25:45).

The essence of Jesus' teaching is given in the Sermon on the Mount, and the essence of that teaching is that God is a God of compassion, and therefore, in all our dealings, our behaviour must be compassionate. That is why we must turn the other cheek, give our cloak as well, walk another mile, love our enemies, do good to those who hate us, bless those who persecute us, because that is the way of God, 'for God himself is kind to the ungrateful and the wicked.' So, St Luke says 'Be compassionate as your Father is compassionate'.(Luke 6:36)

At the Last Supper, Jesus gives final expression to his life's meaning. He takes a piece of bread, blesses it, breaks it and gives it to his friends saying, 'THIS IS ME, GIVEN FOR YOU. DO THIS IN MY MEMORY'. It is as though he were saying, 'This gesture expresses the very essence of my life and of my father's life, that we live to give ourselves to you and for you. . If you are to be one with us, you must let this be the essence of your lives, too, living for one another, not off one another, seeing your lives as a gift given to you so that others may live. That is why I have said to you, "Unless you lose your life, you cannot find it". You are created out of God's love, for God's love, to mirror God's love.'

SOME PRACTICAL CONCLUSIONS

1. The need for private prayer, the prayer experience shared ecumenically
There will be no lasting spiritual renewal in Scotland, or anywhere else, unless it grows out of the prayer life of individuals. Churches in Scotland

provide public worship, public prayers, and exhortations to pray, but there has been, in general, very little teaching on prayer, nor have individuals been encouraged to talk about their own prayer experience. Prayer is about becoming aware of the wealth that is 'closer to us than we are to ourselves'. In Juliana of Norwich's words, 'Utterly at home, God lives in us forever'. There is enormous spiritual wealth in all of us, but the majority of us are not aware of it. Even if we become aware of it, we do not know what to do with it, or how to communicate it. Such is the cultural climate in which we live that we are afraid of talking about our spiritual experience in case we are thought to be odd! If we become aware of the spiritual wealth that is in us, and if we learn how to communicate it, such are the structures of most of our churches that unless we happen to be clergy, we are unlikely to find opportunities to communicate it.

Much teaching on prayer, with its emphasis on 'avoiding distractions', is affected by the split in our spirituality. We need to learn to pray out of ordinary events, situations, things. There is a poem of R.S. Thomas, called 'Emergings', which includes the following:-

> as a form in sculpture is the prisoner
> of the hard rock, so in everyday life
> it is the plain facts and natural happenings
> that conceal God and reveal him to us
> little by little under the mind's tooling.

We need to learn ways of praying which can reveal God to us, not only under the mind's, but also under the heart's tooling. At the end of this article, I offer some ways of praying which allow the events of our day, which is the only place in which we can meet God, to become the substance of our prayer. These are not *THE methods of prayer*. There are as many ways of praying as there are human beings. To those who are not familiar with 'earthed' methods of prayer, these methods can be a useful starting point for you to find your own way of praying.

If people can learn to share their felt experience of prayer with one another, whether in twos or in small groups, preferably of six at the most, the sharing helps us better to understand what happens in our prayer and we are, in some strange way, encouraged and energised by the sharing. We begin to understand better the meaning of Jesus' words, 'where two or three are gathered together in my name, I am there in the midst of them'. After the prayer methods at the end of this article, there are also some brief notes on sharing prayer experience in groups. The groups are not discussion, but sharing groups in which we listen to one another, without any attempt to correct, improve, fix or solve the others' problems! When conducted in this way, the groups are very energising: if they become discussion groups, they soon disintegrate. These groups are especially powerful when the members are from different Christian denominations. This should not surprise us. There is one God, one Spirit given to us all. This Spirit is the Spirit of unity and peace. The unity of the Church will come about through prayer. Without prayer we condemn ourselves to endless committee meetings on unity!

2. Churches always acting together whenever possible
A second practical conclusion is just a reminder of something which has often been said at ecumenical conferences, but which needs constant reminders:

The churches must never do separately what they can possibly do together. This is vitally important. There is one God. When we co-operate, we are nearer to God. It is a wonderful thing to witness the strong bonds of unity which are created among people of different Christian denominations and none, who learn to share with one another their prayer experience. Do this, and you will understand. When we listen to one another, we do not have to agree, nor do we need to compromise our beliefs in any way, but God changes us through our praying and through our listening.

If we pray together across the denominations, the Spirit will make us more perceptive and more responsive to God's promptings, and we shall be moved to live the compassion of God in our own immediate environment and beyond. We shall become more conscious of the needs of those around us, whatever their belief or lack of it.

3. Inter-faith work
A third practical conclusion can be summed up in the words of Canon Max Warren, a former secretary general of the Church Missionary Society, and a man of great experience in inter-faith work:

'Whenever you meet another person of another culture, of another faith, or of no faith, take off your shoes, because you are entering sacred ground: and tread warily, because God has been there before you'.

All the Christians I have met who have engaged in interfaith work, have claimed that the insights they have gained from study and through meeting with people of other faiths, have deepened their understanding and appreciation of their own Christian faith. For peace in our own country and peace in the world, we need to learn to listen to and to respect every human being.

God is in all things. There is no place, no person, no group of people, no aspect of life where God is not. Every bush is burning if only we had the eyes to see. The kingdom of God is essentially inclusive.

4. A model for our time

This is a story, illustrating a spirituality that was very earthed, very simple, very practical, very recognisable by all who encountered it, whether Christian, or of other faiths, or of no faith. *Stella Reekie*, who will be known to many readers, was a Church of Scotland deaconess. At the end of the Second World War, Stella, as a Red Cross nurse, was among the first British to witness the horrors of a German Concentration camp. It was her Damascus experience. After the war she worked with refugees in Europe and in Scotland, then went to Pakistan as a missionary. On retirement to Scotland, she was appointed by the joint Glasgow churches to be a Christian link person with immigrants living in Glasgow. She had a small flat near Glasgow University, which she called 'The International Flat', a microcosm of the U.N. The flat was usually thronging with visitors. Stella would float among them, introducing them to one another, serving them with food, listening to their problems. She did this for many years until she died of cancer. She initiated an inter-faiths exhibition at the McLelland galleries in Glasgow. Her funeral was attended by people of many faiths and none. One of the funeral addresses was given by a Sikh. He said of Stella, 'To us she was like water. She refreshed us, cleansed us, and she assumed the shape of whoever she was with, so that to me she was a Sikh, to my Muslim friends a Muslim, and to my Jewish friends she was Jewish. I have never understood what Christians meant when they said "Jesus died for our sins", but I know that Stella lived and died for us'. What a wonderful tribute to her and to her Christian faith. Her spirituality was not split, but all of a piece. She prayed, but her prayer flowed into her life, pervaded and permeated it, giving her a great warmth and openness, not only with her own immediate circle, but with everyone she encountered, no matter what their race, colour, class, beliefs or lack of them. She had a great love, too, for nature, for the animals, plants and flowers. The compassion of God had so taken hold of her that it seemed completely spontaneous and natural to her. Stella knew her defects and limitations, but that knowledge did not depress her, for her security was not in her own achievements, but in the Spirit at work within and around her. That is why she could be so compassionate, yet so joyful, so dedicated yet so free, a most encouraging example for us all!

APPENDIX I

Some Ways of Praying

WHY PRAY?

Prayer is about meeting with God, but it is also about meeting with ourselves, because 'in God we live and move and have our being'. Our ultimate identity is not in our family, job, or where we live, but in God. Each one of us is a unique manifestation of God. In the Bible, God keeps telling us. 'Don't be afraid, for I am with you'. God loves us unconditionally and God is, in St Augustine's words, 'closer to me than I am to myself'.

Real change in ourselves and in our world has to begin in our minds and hearts, otherwise it will not happen. Prayer is about raising awareness, about seeing our world differently. It is the most revolutionary and liberating activity in which we can engage.

HOW PRAY?

God prays in us. The Spirit, who lived in Jesus and raised him from the dead, now lives in you. So give the Spirit a chance and don't try too hard! Whatever way you pray, and there are as many ways of praying as there are human beings, always be simple, honest, childlike, and pray from the heart to the Heart of God, who loves and cherishes you unconditionally.

'BE STILL AND KNOW THAT I AM GOD' (PSALM 46:10)

On being still. Here is one way:
◆ Sit, feet flat on the ground, back straight but not rigid, body relaxed.
◆ Concentrate your attention on what physically you can feel in your body. Don't think, just attend to what you can feel. You may begin

with your right foot and work upwards. The longer you can spend on one part of the body, the better. No need to cover the syllabus!

u If you feel an itch or discomfort, acknowledge the discomfort but try not to move.

◆ If you become aware of some thoughts or questions, treat them as you treated the itch, acknowledging the thoughts/discomfort, but turning your attention to your physical feelings.

◆ Once you feel rested, you may like to turn this exercise into more explicit prayer, e.g. repeating to yourself the phrase, 'In him I live, and move, and have my being'. Have a conversation with this God. In our awareness of our present experience, we are meeting with God. God, for us, is wherever we happen to be. The only place we can meet God is in our own experience.

PRAYING FROM SCRIPTURE
1. How Start?
◆ With a stillness exercise of some kind.

2. What Then
◆ Our minds can stray all over the place when we begin to pray, so it is good to start with this prayer: 'God, let my whole being be directed totally to your service and praise'.

◆ Read over the Scripture passage on which you are going to pray. Choose a short passage, and one that appeals to you.

◆ Imagine the words of Scripture being spoken to you personally by God at this moment. The God of Scripture is the God who is holding you in being at this moment, and is continuing God's story in you, now! If you are praying with a Gospel passage, see the scene, not just as a spectator, but as an active participant. Meet and interact with the other characters in the scene, and talk with them, especially with Jesus.

◆ Pray for whatever it is you desire. This is important: it focuses your heart.

◆ Consider the passage, pausing to relish and reflect on any words, phrases or images which strike you in any way. Hear the words being spoken to you now by God, and talk to him about them. When what are called 'distractions' – thoughts, memories, imaginings come into your mind which seem to have nothing to do with God or prayer, for example – your own hopes/fears about the future, your relations with others etc., acknowledge these thoughts, memories, imaginings; and as long as you can show them to God, discuss them with God, then stay with them. By doing this you are 'earthing' your prayer, finding God in the details of life. Always speak to God simply, honestly, from your heart, and don't be afraid to grumble. God is big enough to take our tantrums!

◆ If you are praying a Gospel scene, imagine the scene is happening now, and you are in it as you. You do not have to turn yourself into a Palestinian of two thousand years ago! Interact with the characters. It can help you to focus on the scene if you ask yourself, 'who is present, what are they doing, what are they saying?'

◆ Have a conversation with God/Jesus/the Holy Spirit/Mary. There is no need to keep the conversation until the end of your prayer time: the conversation may begin early in your prayer and continue throughout.

◆ End with an 'Our Father' or some other prayer.

REFLECTION AFTER PRAYER

When you have finished praying, it is good to spend a few minutes in reflection. What words, phrases, images struck you? What did you feel during and after the prayer? Did you feel happy/sad, peaceful/agitated, hopeful/anxious? And what gave rise to these feelings? This is what you can share later with others in the group, or with a prayer companion. Through your sharing and listening to others you will begin to see more clearly that whatever happens in prayer reflects, in some way, what is happening in your everyday life, and that the God you meet in prayer is the God who is in all things and in all people.

REVIEW OF THE DAY

This is a method of praying at the end of each day. The events of the day become the subject matter of your prayer, because it is in those events that we are meeting with God.

◆ Be relaxed and ask God, 'Let my whole being be directed to your praise and service'. Let the day play back to you in any order. Look first at what you have enjoyed, appreciated, valued in the day. Relive those moments. They are God's gift to you, signs of God's love. Avoid any self-judgement or moralising: just give thanks for whatever you are grateful. These events are gifts given to you by God, tokens of God's wanting to share God's life with you.

◆ Pray for enlightenment, to recognise God in all the events of the day. To do this, look at your moods and feelings during the day, but without judging them; moods and inner feelings normally arise from our desires, and our permanent desires become attitudes. When our desires are satisfied, we are content: when they are frustrated, we become irritable. We are praying to know the desires and attitudes which underly our moods and feelings. Are my desires directed to God's kingdom — to love, justice, truth, compassion etc., or are they directed to my personal kingdom, my security, my comfort, my success, my wanting creation to praise, reverence and serve me?

◆ Express sorrow if you find you have not been responding to God in the events of the day and beg forgiveness, knowing that God always welcomes and forgives. Thank God, too, for the times you have responded to God's goodness.

◆ Ask God's guidance for tomorrow and entrust yourself to God's goodness, 'like a child in its mother's arms'. (Psalm 131:2)

APPENDIX 11

GUIDELINES FOR SHARING PRAYER EXPERIENCE IN GROUPS

a. General guidelines

◆ Groups, normally six people, decide together where and how frequently they are going to meet, e.g. once a week/fortnight/month.

◆ It is good to have a set time for meetings, e.g. 90 minutes, starting punctually and ending strictly on time. If you decide to meet in one another's houses and the host wishes to offer hospitality, then let it be very simple, e.g. tea/coffee/biscuits, not an elaborate party.

◆ The meetings are for LISTENING and for sharing your felt experience during and after prayer: they are NOT DISCUSSION GROUPS for problem solving.

Let each share in so far as they are willing, their own experience during and after prayer, and let the others listen, but without interruption or comment.

After each has spoken, there may be more from your felt experience that you would like to share, and so the conversation continues, but it is rooted in felt experience.

Feelings are important signals. If some word, phrase, image arouses strong feelings within us, it means that word/phrase is very important for our life's journey, and it needs to be looked at and prayed over again. God communicates with us through our feelings. Through putting our feelings into words and being listened to, we can begin to understand them more clearly. In listening to one another, avoid at all costs any attempt to advise, instruct, correct, criticise, or to sort anyone out!

◆ Whatever is shared in these groups must be treated in confidence.

b. Guidelines for the chairperson.

◆ Invite each member of the group to assist in ensuring that the guidelines are kept. It is good to let each member of the group chair the monthly meeting in turn, if they are willing.

◆ Ensure that anyone who wants to speak has the chance to do so. Allow a short pause after each has spoken. This is both a mark of respect and it improves the listening.

◆ Gently restrain anyone who theorises, lectures, criticises, advises or seems to be trying to sort out the rest of the group, or any individual within it.

◆ Ensure that the formal part of the meeting ends at the time agreed beforehand.

◆ Ensure that everyone knows the time, place and agreed topic for prayer before the next meeting, and appoint a chairperson for it.

CHAPTER SIX

BREAKING INTO PARTNERSHIP WITH SCIENCE AND TECHNOLOGY

Science and Technology: the growth of knowledge in an uncertain world
John Eldridge

One task of human thought is to try to perceive what the range of possibilities may be in a future that always carries on its back the burden of the present and the past. Though that is not the only task of the intellectual it is a very important and very difficult one. No one can do it with complete success. Only those with a religious conviction of the infallibility of their own beliefs can take seriously the notions of inevitable catastrophe and inevitable utopia. To give up such consolations is to become really serious about a very deadly and very serious world.[1]

I write this essay from the standpoint of a sociologist. This is not so much a claim or a confession but simply an indication of where I am coming from. In particular, it is a signal that the notes and queries which follow will want to consider science and technology in a social context. And, so far as the contemporary scene is concerned, that context is one of rapid change with fears and hopes as to what science and technology can deliver. Embedded in all this are ethical issues: the 'ought' questions which seek to address not only what can or might be done through science and technology, but should be done, with what limits and in what circumstances. The answers to these questions are often highly contested. Given that we live in a plural society with competing values this, in itself, is not surprising. Moreover, there are many uncertainties which can cloud discussion such that even people with the same value position may not be in agreement as to what is to be done. Some of these are inherently social and economic in character. The complexities of globalisation can heighten the sense of uncertainty, such that we may have a feeling of powerlessness in a 'runaway world'. It is but a short step to fatalistic conclusions that things are out of control and nothing can be done about it. I want to argue, in the words of the old song, 'it ain't necessarily so'.

SOME PRELIMINARIES.

For many purposes, rightly, we think of science as a modern activity. However, it is salutary to think about science as a way of trying to understand and explain the physical and social universe and how that approach to obtaining knowledge emerged. The noted philosopher of science, Karl Popper, saw the origins of science in the way people began to critically discuss myths, which had offered all kinds of stories about the origin and workings of the universe. It offered a different kind of story telling based on an evolving tradition of critical argument that finds its most well known philosophical expression in Socrates.[2] It was Heraclitus, Popper pointed out, who famously argued that everything is in flux including the very building material of which the earth is made and the artefacts which we produce, and Aristotle who stated that all things are in motion all the time even though we may not always be aware of it. This puts two problems before us. How do we explain change and what kind of knowledge enables us to do this given that it is not immediately apprehended through the senses? From this Popper sets out his view of the scientific tradition as rooted in conjecture and refutation and he cites Heraclitus with approval: 'He who does not expect the unexpected will not detect it; for him it will remain undetectable and unapproachable'.[3] The knowledge that is garnered and the explanations – the theories – that are propounded are always provisional. Thus we have the paradox of scientific knowledge, which grows but is never absolute in its search for truth. What from some perspectives can be seen as the most reliable form of knowledge carries within it an inherent provisionality. Uncertainty is an ever present companion on the scientific journey.

It was the French sociologist, Durkheim, who a century ago argued that the fundamental categories of thought and science itself had religious origins. For him it was religious ideas and mythologies which replaced accounts of the world that relied purely on the senses and, in doing so, created ideals. They arose from within society but also helped to transform them. Moreover, connections were made between the natural world and the social world, as expressed in totemism, rites and ceremonial activities. Unexpected connections were made and a world of symbols was generated. This made possible the development of logical thought and the emergence of ways of thinking about causality. As Durkheim put it:

> As soon as man became aware that internal connections exist between things, science and philosophy became possible. Religion made a way for them. To make men take control of sense impressions and replace them with a new way of imagining the real, a new kind of thought had to be created: collective thought. If collective thought alone had the power to achieve this, here is the reason: Creating a whole world of ideals, through which the world of sensed realities seemed transfigured, would require a hyperexcitation of intellectual forces that is only possible in and through society.[4]

Through the development of concepts a practice of abstraction is made possible such that, so to speak, invisible qualities as well as visible can be imagined. But the cosmologies which are linked with religious thoughts may come to be supplanted by scientific cosmologies. These different cosmologies, or world views, could have implications for the moral order and the ways in which we define ourselves in relation to one another. Although Durkheim argues that religious and scientific thought derive from the same source, we can also see that there may be sources of tension between differing cosmologies, as Galileo's conflict with the Catholic Church and Darwin's evolutionary theory illustrates.

If the concepts we invent and deploy and indeed the language we use to encode them are forms of social classification we can see why sociologists have come to write about the social construction of reality.[5] There is a metaphor here, of course. If reality is socially constructed it is a process of building. Once it is constructed it takes on a life of its own, over and above us. But the building may be added to, modified, even, although usually with difficulty, destroyed. It is a human activity *par excellence*, usually a collective one. That is why we find sociologists writing about the social construction of religion[6] and of science.[7] But although this may be seen as scandalous by some involved in the practice of religion and/or science, they only represent a more general tendency, as Hacking points out in his nicely titled '*The Social Construction of What?*'[8] To pick out from an endless list of instances: knowledge, gender, post-modernism, nationalism and facts have all been written about as socially constructed. What, we might pause to wonder, does this do for our concept of objectivity (is that socially constructed?) of nature (another candidate) not to mention questions of causality and the 'things' in our world and universe which may exist independently of our knowing about them? Are not the shadows of relativism all around us, with all their cognitive and ethical uncertainties?

And what about technology? As a species we are tool-making and tool-using and it is salutary to think of the simple tools of paleo-lithic and neo-lithic societies in contrast to the complexity of modern computer and digital technology. Our productive activities call forth technical skills and represent an application of knowledge to achieving tasks and tackling problems. It is not just technology as material artefacts but the ways in which human beings relate to them that is of interest to the sociologist. Indeed, technology does not just refer to particular implements but to productive systems which are linked to human activities – designs, plans, choices and decisions as to what uses technology will be deployed. At which point we are likely to speak of technological systems and start to ask questions about who is in control. Technology is a social product, an outcome of human knowledge and, we may suggest, related to human ideas, ideals and interests. This is the reason why it is possible to think of technology as socially shaped. While modern technology makes many things possible for us and affects us in many ways in our lives, we do not conclude that everything is driven by it: in other words that modern societies are determined by technology. If it were so we would be the victims of what we had created, which is the stuff of some pessimistic science fiction novels. But issues of politics, economics and culture are part of the fabric of modern societies with their values and interests impinging on what gets done and what does not. There is no easy answer to the question 'what drives what' in the constellations and configurations that are produced and reproduced.

In modern societies we tend to think of technology as closely connected with, even an application of, science. But, as Mackenzie and Wajcman have pointed out, significant inventions such as the water-mill, the spinning jenny and the steam engine were not really based on the application of science to technology. And, where there is a connection, it can sometimes work both ways:

> Technology has arguably contributed as much to science as vice versa – think of the great dependence of science on the computer, without which some modern scientific specialities could scarcely have come into existence. Most importantly, where technology does draw on science, the nature of the relation is not one of technologists passively deducing the 'implications' of scientific advance. Technology, as the word's etymology reminds us, is knowledge as well as artefacts, and the knowledge deployed by engineers is far from just applied science . . .. Engineers *use* science. They seek from science resources to

help them solve the problems they have, to achieve the goals towards which they are working. These problems and goals are at least as important in explaining what they do as the science that is available for them to use.[9]

SOME PROBLEMS NOTED

1. THE PROBLEM OF MODERNITY. The story of modernity can be told in a number of different ways. But a common version has to do with the rise of industrial societies, which are closely connected to the growth of science and technology. If the Enlightenment signified the emphasis on reason in guiding human affairs, the application of knowledge to harnessing the forces of nature for the purposes of human welfare, the development of the wealth of nations and the liberty of the individual, then the story of modernity was the story of human progress. Science and technology could be seen as the servants, the instruments of this grand narrative. In medicine, in food production, in transport, in industry – in all spheres of human activity the story was one of modernisation. Transformations in the economic sphere were accompanied by transformations in the political sphere. So it was that capitalism was linked with the growth of democracy and the story could be told sometimes with a flourish of triumphalism. Democracy, after all, was the jewel in the crown of political development: the people would be no more subjects but participating citizens able to take part in the shaping of their own future.

However, from the beginning there was always a dark side to the story of modernity. If we think about modern times in relation to collision of the 'old world' (Europe) with the 'new world' (the Americas) then the story begins in tragedy and something approaching genocide. To some extent this part of story was repressed by the enlightenment emphasis on reason and the 'rights of man'. The story was to develop in relation to colonisation and the growth of modern empires. Whatever benefits emerged from the imposition of colonial rule it was grounded first and last in military power, summed up in the couplet:

> Whatever happens we have got
> the maxim gun and they have not.

Other parts of the dark side of the story could not be repressed. The wars of the twentieth century pockmarked the earth and its peoples in unimaginably terrible ways. Yet these were times when science and technology developed new kinds of knowledge and applications in weaponry, on land, sea and air; the secrets of the atom were prised open and applied to Hiroshima and Nagasaki; the possibilities of biological warfare were explored. The space race of the Cold War period always had military dimensions. Today the so-called Star Wars scenario is back on the political agenda of the USA. The part that geo-politics has played in the construction of 'big science' and the institutional complexes that have arisen to support it can scarcely be underestimated.

The relationship between capitalism and democracy was, after all, not so clear cut. First of all the emergence of communism and the formation of the Soviet Union offered an alternative vision of the modernity story with a strong emphasis on forced industrialisation. For Lenin this great leap forward would have to be achieved through electrification and Taylorist methods of production. The United States was both the ideological enemy and the technological model to emulate. But in place of the capitalist market came the state plan. The fate of the Soviet Union under Stalin has by now been well documented. The role of scientists and technologists was a functional one. They were subordinated to the party and the state at times, as the infamous Lysenko case demonstrated, to the detriment of science itself.

Secondly, there is the phenomenon of fascism, which in Hitler's Germany and Mussolini's Italy co-existed with capitalism. Its outworking of a racist vision led to the concentration camps and the holocaust. It serves as a devastating lesson of the instrumental purposes to which science can be put when it is turned into ideology – the ideology of racism based on spurious anthropology. One of the most significant books produced by a contemporary sociologist is Zygmunt Bauman's ' *Modernity and the Holocaust*'. In it he argues:

> The Holocaust was born and executed in our modern rational society, at the high stage of our civilisation and at the peak of human cultural achievement, and for this reason it is a problem of that society, civilisation, and culture. (author's italics). The self-healing of historical memory which occurs in the consciousness of modern society is for this reason more than a neglect offensive to the victims of the genocide. It is also a sign of dangerous and potentially suicidal blindness.[10]

What Bauman underlines is that the extermination of very large numbers of human beings was accomplished in a way that could only take place in conditions of modernity. He is referring to the social technology of rational bureaucracies with their efficient (compared to earlier forms) organisations, filing and precision. This was co-ordinating the transport, the construction of gas chambers, the disposal of bodies and effects. It was a particular application of instrumental rationality. It entailed discipline, order and routine: there was a hierarchical division of labour. Problems of a technical nature, such as the design of vehicles, were for solving in their own terms and not with reference to human values. It was an application of the principles of social engineering. In the process 'moral invisibility' was produced.

> The technical-administrative success of the Holocaust was due in part to the skilful utilization of "moral sleeping pills" made available by modern bureaucracy and modern technology. The natural invisibility of causal connections in a complex system of interaction, and the distancing of the unsightly or morally repelling outcomes of action to the point of rendering them invisible to the actor, were most prominent among them. Yet the Nazis particularly excelled (in) . . .the method of making invisible the very humanity of the victims . . .To render the humanity of victims invisible, one needs merely to evict them from the universe of obligation.[11]

There is then, for Bauman, a very great lesson to be learned. If the Holocaust was 'at home' in the house of modernity, what else might come to inhabit the place in the name of instrumental rationality? If this awareness of the destructive tendencies within modernity is silenced or blunted we will lack the moral resources to confront and overcome them. The house of modernity can become the prison house, or in Weber's celebrated phrase, an 'iron cage'. Instrumental rationality can be used to pursue many purposes. This, I think, was what informed Marcuse's once famous essay on industrialisation and capitalism, which disturbingly suggested that technology itself is not neutral.

> Not only its application but technique itself is domination (over nature and men), methodological, scientific, calculated and calculating control. Certain aims and interests of control are not "additional" or externally dictated to technique – they are intrinsic to the construction of the technical apparatus itself: technique is a historical and social project: in it is projected what a society and its ruling interests decide to make of men and things. Such an "aim" of domination is material to the form of technical reason itself.[12]

2. THE PLACE OF SCIENCE AND TECHNOLOGY IN A 'RISK SOCIETY'. The German sociologist Ulrich Beck has made a significant contribution to the discussion on the role of science and technology in the modern world.[13] It flows from his contention that what is new in the modern period is the way risk is produced as a consequence of industrialisation. The risks, some of which are now global, were for the most part unanticipated and unintended. Because of the way in which the earth's resources have been worked upon in the modern period, extensively and intensively, we can no longer think of nature as outside of society or society as outside of nature. It is the very widespread development of threats to nature from culture (routinised ways of life and activity) which leads him to promote the concept of 'risk society'. It is the globalised nature of the threats and their modern causes that make them distinctively modern He refers, for example to radio-activity, to toxins and pollutants in the air, the water and foodstuffs and to the short and long term effects these have on plants, animals and people. The human interventions that have led to this might be described as the manufacture of uncertainties. As these risks become recognised and defined, even while their significance may be hotly debated, attempts are made to manage risk in terms of trying in systematic ways to deal with hazards and insecurities that have been induced by modernisation itself. The threats to the human species and the planet itself, set alongside the awareness that something must be done, is for Beck what characterises this period of late modernity.

Since these unintended consequences have arisen out of rational attempts to control and domesticate nature for human purposes, we might imagine that Beck propounds an anti-scientific manifesto and takes up an anti-Enlightenment position. But it is not so. Nor does he take up a post-modern position by arguing that there are no grand narratives left for us to live by because fragmentation and a runaway world are all that is left. To recognise the problems is for him the beginning of wisdom and to consider what might be done and how, is the challenge of our times. We need more reason not less. Thus he argues: 'To me the Enlightenment is *not* a historical notion and set of ideas but a process and a dynamics where criticism, self-criticism, irony and humanity play a central role . . .I argue for the opening up to democratic scrutiny of the previously depoliticised realms of decision-making.'[14] This is a very demanding project and sometimes pessimism will dominate discussion but ultimately for Beck this represents a way of confronting organised irresponsibility and offers the possibility of moving beyond it. But the concept of organised irresponsibility is not just an empirical label but a moral one. It has an ethical dimension. Too often this dimension has been hidden by the pragmatic and expedient considerations of one interest group or another. We might think of the recovery of this dimension as the return of the repressed.

DILEMMAS AND QUERIES.

I. IS SCIENCE THE DISINTERESTED USE OF KNOWLEDGE? The idea that knowledge is pursued for its own sake and that it is then put into the public domain for critical discussion is increasingly problematical. That of course was one of the traditional bases for claims to the authority and legitimacy of science and scientists. Not only so, but it could carry with it the image of the individual, independent scientist fearlessly and single-mindedly pursuing truth. Today, the institution of science is typically organised in bureaucratic organisations – some employed and funded by government, some by commercial enterprises, including multi-national corporations. And universities, while they may be engaged in basic as well as applied science, are themselves entwined in government and commercial funding arrangements. It is not news to say that 'whoever pays the piper calls the tune' and therefore questions as to whom the science and its applications are for need to stay on the agenda. The organisation of science (and technology) can therefore shape what is selected as a problem, what is funded and the extent to which its results are disseminated. At its worst we can see the way the image of the scientist is used in advertising: we are encouraged to buy something because 'scientists' tell us it is good for us in some way or other. This may be linked to professional advice – dentists may assure us that a drink does no harm to our teeth according to 'research findings' – or governmental advice that despite the presence of BSE in cattle, beef is safe to eat – or industrial assurances that nuclear power plants are very low risk places. The social, economic and political contexts within which science is done can never be taken for granted. Each organisation which has its own interests in the outcomes of scientific research and its potential applications will have its own agenda and aims and a set of values which these express. How this works out in practice, what is negotiable, what priorities are established with what funding will give us a strong clue as to the nature of the power relations which surround that activity.

2. WHO ARE THE SCIENTIFIC AND TECHNOLOGICAL EXPERTS?
Given the vast numbers of scientists and technologists who are now

employed in the world, we might suppose that there is no shortage of them. Even so, given the detailed specialisation that now takes place, even those of us who lay claim to being experts might in practice have a very limited domain of expertise. In that sense most of us are lay people about most things scientific. As for the experts themselves they can disagree about the significance or implications of particular scientific and technological developments. But, Anthony Giddens has pointed out: 'Even in fields where experts are in a consensus, because of the shifting and developing nature of modern knowledge, the 'filter-back effects on lay thought and practice will be ambiguous and complicated. The risk element of modernity is thus unsettling for everyone; no-one escapes.'[15] In terms of the politics of such a situation this is a reminder of how a democratic deficit can be created and extended if experts are not made accountable and if their claims are not subject to scrutiny and made accessible for dialogue with an informed citizenry. The reference to an informed citizenry is a reminder of the importance of education in such a process. Without it the ability to critique and evaluate what is taking place is diminished. This is one way of reminding ourselves of the importance of civil society and that vigilance is the price of democratic freedom, which can never be taken for granted. Indeed it has been argued that 'the sovereignty with which technical decisions are made and justified on other than technological grounds is one measure of democracy'.[16]

3. WHAT IS THE RELATIONSHIP BETWEEN POWER AND RESPONSIBILITY IN SCIENCE AND TECHNOLOGY? There is not, and we would not expect to find, one simple answer to this broad question. But let us take one area which is full of controversy and explore it a little: bio-technology. Crick and Watson's discovery at Cambridge University of the structure of DNA created a new scientific paradigm that has had revolutionary consequences. It has given rise to 'the new genetics'. Since then many applications have been attempted that have relevance for the practice of medicine and agriculture and have impinged directly or indirectly upon life itself – plant, animal and human. It has given rise to what we now routinely call 'genetic engineering'. The term is worth pondering. As a result of new knowledge it is possible to work with animate materials, dis-aggregating things that were formerly connected, re-assembling them with other materials so that something new is constituted from hitherto unavailable possibilities. There is, in other words, a breaking down, manipulation and the creation of new assemblages. As with other developments such as nuclear power and information technology, genetic engineering has become a highly significant sphere of activity. Its applications generate hopes and fears. Ironically, in the light of my preliminary comments, two contradictory myths about science and scientists can be observed. There is the myth of the all-powerful scientist, who can guide us into a better future by bringing manifold benefits and solving the problems of disease and hunger. But there is also the Frankenstein myth: science has brought irreversible changes into our world such that we are now in thrall of powerful forces outside our control. The first carries with it connotations of trust; the second signifies suspicion. Since we are in an area which deals with the science and technology of creation we might well understand the feelings of ambivalence that are represented but it is paradoxical that science, which sought to supersede mythological accounts of the world, has not been able to prevent the emergence of powerful myths about its own practice.

We have seen the controversies surrounding the work on genetically modified organisms (GMOs). They are multi-stranded. In the field of agriculture there are questions of patenting, of what constitutes safe experimentation, of how the precautionary principle should be applied. At its broadest there are those who argue that since this is a way forward to dealing with world hunger properly regulated field experiments must be allowed; others argue that the human species has become the subject of experimentation. Most of us, for better or worse, consciously or unknowingly have consumed GMO food. The big trans-national corporations are at the centre of much of this. The near monopolistic position of such powerful companies, their concern with commercial secrecy and their need to generate profit for their shareholders makes them subject to criticism from consumer groups and environmental activists. We have somehow to try and see 'the big picture' whilst recognising how multi-layered the issues are. Donna Haraway nicely encapsulates this:

> . . . a seed contains inside its coat the history of practices such as collecting, breeding, marketing, taxonomising, patenting, biochemically analysing, advertising, eating, cultivating, harvesting, celebrating, and starving. A seed produced in the biotechnological institutions now spread around the world contains the specifications for labour systems, planting calendars, pest control procedures, marketing, land-holding, and beliefs about hunger and well being.[17]

At the time of writing much publicity surrounds the announcement of 'the book of humankind', the results of the human genome project. In fact there have been two competing groups of scientists working on the deciphering of the human genome. One was the international consortium of scientists funded by public money and charities; the other a privately funded American based group. There have been all too human arguments about methodologies, 'borrowing' and who stole whose thunder. But crucially the question of access to the findings has been at issue. The public consortium's data has always been freely available to everyone. The position of the privately funded group is more equivocal. This is indeed an ethical issue. As Dr. Mike Dexter of the Wellcome Trust put it: 'Imagine the problem for chemistry if the periodic table was in a private data bank and you were charged for access. That would be incredibly stupid.'[18] While there are not always easy answers we do need to consider that ethical issues thread through the whole process from funding, to access, to patenting, to ownership, to control and to distribution. It is when these matters are explicitly attended to, which may involve the creation of and support for international as well as national regulating agencies that we can begin to re-connect power with responsibility. This also, I suspect, is one element in building trust between the public and those who offer us the fruits of science and technology.

AN ECUMENICAL EXPERIMENT IN PARTNERSHIP: THE SOCIETY, RELIGION AND TECHNOLOGY PROJECT.

In May 1970, the Church of Scotland appointed Dr. John Francis, an Anglican, as the first Director of the newly formed Society, Religion and Technology Project. (SRT) He was a scientist working in the field of nuclear energy. An account of the work of the project by Ronald Ferguson was published in 1994, entitled '*Technology at the Crossroads*'. Although the setting up of this project involved the efforts of a number of people, reference is properly made to Dr. William Robertson who, in a speech at the University of Strathclyde in March 1968 made the case for trying to bridge the gap as he saw it between theologians and scientists, between church and industry. This was effectively a foundation document for setting up the project. To read the speech is to be seized by his sense of concern and urgency. He emphasised the rapidity of change in society brought about by technological invention, now so great that it had brought about an entirely new situation: 'This is an explosion of change. If you think I exaggerate, the truth is that I am not capable of stating the true character of the situation with sufficient force and urgency. The history of the development of man and his society is a history of his inventions and the changes they make possible. So an explosive, almost limitless growth of his power of invention – and that is what we are witnessing – will produce explosive changes in society, in institutions, in the whole outlook on life. The signs are all around us.'[19]

The challenge to the church was clear to Robertson:

> I am asking three questions. Who is looking forward to the shape of industrial things to come ? Who is saying . . ."Let us act in God's name to avoid this in the future or to achieve that ?" Who has learned from the past fifty years that the ordinary human dynamic, geared to the new technological dynamism, does not in some automatic way create a world in which God's will is done, but rather shapes a world in which it is increasingly difficult for God's will to be done? It is to questions like these that no reply comes out of the silence.[20]

What kind of partnership was it that came into being with the SRT project? Firstly, although established by the Church of Scotland from which it still gets its core funding, the steering committee, which meets on a regular basis with the Director has always been ecumenical in composition. The membership of the steering committee includes clergy and lay people. (Here I declare an interest as a member of that committee). There is an academic input from different disciplines and contributions from people directly involved in the practice of science and technology. The agenda for work to be done is formed in continuing conversation with the Director and the steering committee, although the Director who brings to the project particular skills, experience and scientific knowledge, plays a key role in deciding what is to be done.

Secondly, the Director has had to sustain credibility in scientific, governmental and management circles. Involvement in this secular sphere is crucial. There is a task of communication between the church and the world which the Director has to seek to facilitate. This is not a matter of simple compliance with the governmental or industrial powers that be. The first Director was himself involved in the British Society for Social Responsibility in Science, set up by scientists Hilary and Stephen Rose, which was a secular group of scientists constantly raising questions as to the application of science in such areas as military weaponry, eugenics, with concerns about human costs and benefit always in view. That group no longer exists but there is today another similar group, Scientists for Global Responsibility, which does raise ethical questions about scientific and technological development.

Thirdly, there has been a style of work which has involved collaboration with scientists and those from other disciplines. For example, under the leadership of the then Director, Dr. Howard Davis, a multi-disciplinary, ecumenical group met regularly to discuss the ways in which science and technology was embedded in defence strategy. This was in the early eighties, when nuclear strategy was much debated and when the peace movement in Europe was a considerable force. The group, which was by no means always agreed, made a point not only of listening to one another but to people representing different viewpoints and positions – members of the 'peace movement' as well as NATO officials who were visited *in situ*. The eventual publication, *Ethics and Defence*[21] represented a serious and sustained attempt to consider the ways in which questions of technology and politics were interwoven with ethical questions.

In the last few years, under the Directorship of Dr. Donald Bruce, a nuclear physicist, a group of geneticists at the leading edge of their subject met with him, two social scientists, an animal breeding specialist and an ethicist. The purpose was to discuss the ethics of genetic engineering in non-human species. This involved regular meetings over several years. The group itself had to develop trust among its members given the sensitive nature of some of the issues and the differences of opinion that sometimes emerged. This initiative provided a space for regular meetings in which questions could be explored that in the busy professional routine could often be ignored or dealt with in a limited way. This led to the publication of *Engineering Genesis*[22] which, it is fair to say, has been a critical success. From within the green movement and from industry and the academy, the work has been accepted as a serious, thoughtful investigation of the issues. A second edition is now being worked on. This kind of partnership takes time, but it is one way of earning the right to speak on these complex matters. The openings that this has given to the director of SRT have ranged from debates at the Oxford Union with Richard Dawkins, to meetings with policy makers in Britain, Europe and the USA, as well as many opportunities in press and broadcasting. This kind of partnership is hard earned but it is surely worth the effort. The SRT project offers us a model in partnership of what can be achieved with relatively slender resources. There is now some welcome support from other churches. There is so much more that could be done.

Looking back at a project which has now been in existence for over thirty years we can see that some of its work anticipated issues that later became the subject of widely debated concern. To use concepts such as 'the sustainable society' as early as the 1970s was, suggested John Francis, an indication that 'the Project was in the right place at the right time contributing to the formation and communication of ideas both inside the Church and beyond.'[23] There is something of a prophetic role which is being performed here. We can see this again in work which has emerged about the impact of science and technology on the environment. An SRT publication, *While the Earth Endures*,[24] included some reflections by the theologian Ruth Page. She pointed out that in theological discussion the earth was often viewed simply in instrumental terms – what we can get out of it and from it. She went on to distinguish between ideas of stewardship, trusteeship and companionship. The last of these is particularly innovating and represents a different perspective on partnership. She writes:

> The role of companion excludes the possibility of adversarial tactics with nature – that attitude of confrontation and control which was thought until recently to be an essential part of the "scientific method". Instead, companionship involves a dialogue to-and-fro between humanity's interest and nature's. There is a sense in which companionship thus exercised is a fulfilment of the command to love our neighbours as ourselves – our neighbours being in this case our neighbourhood, our environment. The existence of that relationship prevents any powerful take-over on the part of that humanity. Humans can defend themselves from nature's advances, but nature cannot defend itself so well from humans, so the necessity for respect inherent in companionship is a requirement for humanity alone.[25]

Here, of course, we come to the advocacy of certain values as against other possibilities. A stance to life is commended. It is an aspiration which manifestly is a long way from fulfilment. But then so is the gospel which Christians offer. Moreover, as Ronald Ferguson writes at the end of *Technology at the Crossroads*,

> So much theology has cut itself off from the characteristics of the person of Jesus – from his gentleness, his servanthood, his refusal of the way of domination and violence, his radically new conception of the nature of religious authority, his compassion, his lack of concern over status, his co-operation with the Father, his love of nature, and his concern with community. It is curious

how often these features are entirely absent from any discussion of how human beings are intended to behave – as if the earthly Jesus of Nazareth were simply a fleshly vehicle for an ethereal theological "Christ" who could get on with the real heavyweight work of redemption.[26]

There indeed is a partnership to discover from which so much might spring.

CONCLUSION: SOME MAXIMS.

By way of conclusion I should like to offer a few maxims. They are written first to myself as a result of reflecting on this topic. They are not intentionally provocative but you never can tell!

◆ *Be suspicious of deterministic theories.* One reason for this is that there are quite a number of them and they cannot all be right. We can encounter versions of technological determinism, economic determinism, psychological determinism, biological determinism and now genetic determinism. Sometimes this smacks of a disciplinary imperialism. Such theories often have a reductionist character as in the notion of a gay gene, or a crime gene that are as speculative as they are headline catching. We can come to recognise that there are different levels of explanation and the connections between those levels are of various kinds. Once we come to recognise the distinction there is plenty of room for human agency. Constraint is not determinism.

◆ *Science is not scientism.* Science cannot tell us how to live. But the dogma of scientism pretends to tell us that it can. Like all dogmas it can be fashioned in various ways. A classic case was scientific socialism; another springs from applying some form of Darwinian theory to judgments as to how society should be run as a form of the survival of the fittest. This takes us on the motorway to ideology. Since Hume we should have been sensitive to the difference between the 'is' and the 'ought'. This distinction has considerable implications when it comes to considerations of the relationship between science and public policy.

◆ *Don't demonise.* This is not easy. Debates about scientific and technological issues can become adversarial. This is not surprising since much can hang on outcomes. The debates may operate at various levels – methodological, empirical, political, ethical. But when we demonise 'the other' we stop listening. It is not always easy to 'reason together' but all too easy to have stereotyped views of the adversary.

◆ Cultivate media literacy. Most of our information about science and technology comes through the mass media. Consequently it is filtered to us through the news values that are prevalent at the time. There is much interest at the moment in problems relating to the public understanding of science. But this is not just a matter of scientists speaking plain English. Stories about science and technology can be told in very different ways both by scientists and journalists. Journalists may spin a story in relation to their news values so that it is given a value the scientist may not agree with. But news about science can also be packaged by public relations specialists with particular commercial or political purposes in mind. Questions of truth are not straightforward in a world of sometimes competing interpretations. We need to learn not only how to read between the lines, as it were, but to cultivate our own imagination. It is there that our values can come explicitly into focus. Eric Hobsbawm gives us a relevant example concerning world inequalities with which I conclude:

> ' . . . in a world filled with such inequalities, to live in the favoured regions is to be virtually cut off from the experience, let alone the reactions of people outside those regions. It takes an enormous amount of effort of the imagination, as well as a great deal of knowledge, to break out of our comfortable, protected, and self-absorbed enclaves and enter an uncomfortable and unprotected larger world inhabited by the majority of the human species. We are cut off from this world even if the sum total of amassed information is everywhere accessible at the click of a mouse, if images of the remotest parts of the globe reach us at all times of the day and night, if more of us travel between civilisations than ever before. This is the paradox of a globalised twenty-first century.'[27]

CHAPTER SEVEN

BREAKING INTO DYNAMIC WAYS OF BEING CHURCH

John Drane & Olive M Fleming Drane

INTRODUCTION

Lest it be lost in the discussion that follows, we want to make one very important statement right at the outset of this chapter. That is, that we all owe a great debt to those who have preceded us in the community of faith which is the Christian church. Over the past two hundred years in particular, Christians in Scotland have faithfully borne witness to the Gospel in the midst of many complex and challenging circumstances. A hundred years ago, the very possibility of religious belief seemed to hang in the balance, caught between the rock of philosophical rationalism and the hard place of scientific optimism. By the middle of the twentieth century, the voices of social scientists were adding their own bleak predictions, with the assumption that the progress of secularization was unstoppable, and would soon ensure the total extermination of religious belief not only from Western culture, but from the globalized culture which was then only just beginning to emerge.[1] Given all that (and these were by no means the only anti-Christian trends in the wider culture), it is something of a miracle that the church has survived at all, and we owe that to the insight and sheer hard work of generations of believers who went before us. That is not to say that they did not, of course, make some mistakes, nor to imply that, with the benefit of hindsight, it is not possible to see how in some respects they may even have contributed to the decline that the churches have suffered in more recent times. But overall, they were people of integrity who struggled to contextualize the Gospel effectively in the world of which they were a part. In the process, they got many things right, and some things wrong, which is perhaps about as much as any of us can ever hope for. If we are to make progress in our generation it will not be by sniping at what is past, but by looking to the future and recognizing that we too are limited in our perspectives.

None of us can see beyond the immediate present, but there is no doubt that the future will be radically different from the past. Our grandparents were born towards the end of the nineteenth century, and just over a hundred years later we ourselves became grandparents. The world into which our grand-daughter has been born – let alone the world in which she will live out the rest of her life – is radically different from the world of our grandparents. People of their generation did of course witness many remarkable changes in lifestyles and attitudes, but at the end of their lives the world was still fundamentally the same as it had been at the time of their birth. Admittedly, the British Empire had disappeared, and with it much of the triumphant optimism of the Victorian era, but the map of the world had not been so radically redrawn as it was in the final decade of the twentieth century. Domestic life had become progressively easier, but mostly through the mechanization of operations that they would already have been familiar with from their childhood. Health and life expectancy had undergone radical changes for the better, which is why our grandparents lived to more than twice the age that might have been predicted at the time they were born.

But none of us can live now the way our grandparents did. Today, we transport ourselves with greater speed and efficiency than at any previous time in the whole of history, and that affects the sort of places we live and the ways in which we are able to work.

For many people, it is becoming increasingly unnecessary to travel between home and work at all on a regular basis, because so much work can now be done remotely, as it were. Using our computers, we communicate with people on the other side of the world on a daily basis, and think nothing of it. Today as we write this, we have already exchanged instant messages with friends in Australia, Singapore, Africa, and several parts of the USA, as well as the UK, and tomorrow we will repeat the process, quite possibly with even more varied destinations. In the last five years we have been literally round the world four times, with many shorter trips in between. Throughout their entire lives, our grandparents scarcely left the town in which they were raised, and their most significant journeys were undertaken by our grandfathers during service in the army. The way we use our leisure time has undergone a similar transformation. Indeed, our grandparents would probably not have known what 'leisure' was in the sense we think of it today. They certainly would have found our ways of relating to one another quite different from anything they ever experienced. The idea that either of us would be writing a chapter for a book on the church would have been unimaginable, and writing it together would be beyond anything they could comprehend – either in terms of how it might be done, or why we would wish to undertake such a thing. Social class was a key factor that both limited their lives and offered them such opportunities as they enjoyed. Though Britain is still a class-conscious society when compared with some other countries, our expectations of what is possible for all our citizens have been significantly redefined in recent years. Moreover, the shape and structure of our families has all but completely changed in the last twenty years, and definitions of what a family is, and how someone might join a family, continue to evolve.[2]

The church seems to be one of the few areas of life where little has changed. If there is one place where our grandparents might still feel at home, this would perhaps be it. For the most part, our expressions of what it means to be church are merely variations on what was happening a hundred years ago. We still gather in the same way, in some cases even sitting on the same seats. In most churches, we still expect that worship is essentially something for trained clergy to 'conduct', and participation by the worshippers is restricted to the singing of hymns and maybe the occasional 'Amen' at the end of a prayer. Even when changes have been introduced, the vast majority of them are of an essentially cosmetic character. We wear more relaxed styles of clothing, sing some different hymns, play guitars and drums as well as organs, read less of the Bible from more recent translations, use overhead projectors, listen to much shorter sermons, and expect liturgies to be in contemporary English rather than in Latin or the language of Shakespeare. But these are all minor adjustments when compared to other aspects of contemporary church life, and here the reality is that all the most significant changes have not come about by our own choice, but have been forced upon us by what has been happening in the wider culture. Our grandparents would be surprised at how few people now attend church on an average Sunday, not to mention the way in which the numbers of those with any living connection with the church has declined seriously as a proportion of the overall population. They would find it odd that 'regular' attendance could be defined in terms of those who are there once a month, that most church members and attenders are now women (though, paradoxically, most church leaders are still men), that organized worship is now mostly restricted to a single event that takes place for an hour or so on Sunday mornings, and that Sunday Schools have all but disappeared – not because they have been replaced by other catechetical opportunities for children and young people, but because so many churches have few, if any, people under the age of fifty or so.

These facts are all well known, and have been well enough documented elsewhere for it to be unnecessary to include more of them here.[3] We are now called upon to wrestle with the reality of what they represent. For the last forty years, the statistics have reflected an accelerating crisis in church life, and we are now faced with the serious possibility — likelihood, even — that the Christian faith might disappear entirely from our culture within the first half of this century. That certainly seems to be the scenario to which the figures point. Even a more optimistic prognosis suggests that, unless there are some quite fundamental changes, the church's presence will be limited to a decreasing number of urban worship centres, with large parts of the country — including urban as well as rural neighbourhoods — effectively de-churched. If that sounds like a dire prediction, then we should remember the lesson of north Africa, which in the early centuries of the Christian era was home to some of the most significant theologians and churches of the whole of Christian history, and is now totally bereft of any significant Christian presence. Our churches are in incredibly bad shape. Moreover, the decline is affecting all Christian traditions. Every denomination faces the same issues, and they extend right across the theological spectrum.

OPTIMISM AND PESSIMISM

We often wonder why we are still in the church. After all, most of our peers left it long ago — not only those who went to the same schools as we did, but also those with whom John trained for ministry. Very many of them are not only out of ministry but have given up altogether on Christian belief. Quite possibly, a significant number of those reading this in preparation for the Scottish Ecumenical Assembly will be feeling exactly the same way. Three years ago John conducted a survey on attitudes to evangelism among the Scottish churches, the findings of which were subsequently presented to the ACTS Commission on Mission, Evangelism, and Education. Though it is difficult to quantify, a common thread running through many of the responses was the feeling that a lot of churches contain a lot of discouraged and frustrated people. There was a fair amount of anecdotal evidence to suggest that one reason why Christians are apparently reticent to invite others to share their faith is because they are despairing of its effectiveness themselves.

One of the most obvious ways in which this impinges on the lives of so many is the apparent inability of all our churches to nurture their own children from infancy through to a mature adult expression of Christian faith. This is actually one of the biggest challenges we face. It is of course true that many young people in Scotland today have no idea what the Gospel, or the church, is about. But when the children of church members opt out of active involvement in the life of the Christian community, we cannot claim that they are doing so out of misguided ignorance. Those who have been brought up in the church leave, not because they don't understand, but precisely because they do – and what they find in church life lacks the power to speak to them in any meaningful way. Put simply, many of those people who have stayed with the church into mid-life are now having to face the uncomfortable fact that it seems as if it hasn't worked for their own families – so how can they with integrity invite others to become a part of it? When you place these facts alongside the statistics of church decline, they raise some far-reaching questions, for it appears that – even at this late stage – if we were able to nurture our own children effectively, the numerical decline of our churches would be halted overnight, and might even be turned into growth.

There is no denying that words like 'crisis' are entirely justified to describe the circumstances in which we now find ourselves, and no useful purpose will be served by trying to redefine that in some way that might appear to be less challenging. This is why we make no apology for calling us here to a realistic appraisal of the struggle that we face. But it is also important for us to sound a note of optimism. To varying degrees, both of us have a broadly optimistic outlook about most things in life. Our individual temperaments are well suited, and predispose us to tend to look on the bright side and to expect good outcomes rather than bad. But there is more reason than that for being an optimist as far as the church is concerned. At the risk of being labelled naive or pietistic by some of you, we are going to say that we think the church has a future because it is rooted in God. Though the church is, of course, a social organization, that is not all that we are called to be. It is not even our primary calling, for as the people of God, our life and witness needs to have a transcendent dimension to it. Any discussion about the church and its future will always run the risk of spending too much time talking about ourselves, and too little reflecting on the mystery that is God. Could it be that, up to this point, we have put rather too much faith in ourselves and too little trust in the grace of God?

Another reason for optimism, not unconnected with that, is the way in which the church has grown exponentially in the non-western world in recent decades. Today, almost 70% of the world's Christians are non-white, non-western people.[4] There are many complexities involved in understanding what is going on in this shift of the church's centre of gravity away from the West, but at the very least it must make available to us a vast wealth of insight and experience that should both inspire and inform us in our own concern to re-evangelize Scotland. This is really what our agenda will have to be: how can we transform ourselves from being churches for those who are already members, into churches that will have mission at their heart?

One of the other encouraging features of our day is that increasing numbers of us are asking that question. In recent years, most of our denominations have launched their own programmes and training schemes to try to do something about effecting that change, though from what we can see such progress as we have made has been fragmented and half-hearted. At denominational level, none of our churches has really succeeded in making the paradigm shift from maintenance to mission. But that does not mean we have not changed. Whether we recognize it or not, the church is changing already, not always in positive and life-giving ways. We cannot insulate ourselves from the huge social changes that are going on all around us, and the real question is not, 'Will our churches change?' but 'What kind of change will affect our churches?' More precisely, will we sit back and allow ourselves to be changed by whatever might be happening in the wider culture, or are we prepared to take the initiative to become ourselves the divinely empowered agents for change that will truly make a difference, not only in our own lives but in the life of the world more widely? This debate is not about being trendy, nor is it really about being relevant. It is about being incarnational.

MODERNITY, POSTMODERNITY, AND CULTURAL CHANGE

What then might be involved in contextualizing the Gospel in the emerging postmodern culture? At the conclusion of his book *The Death of Christian Britain*, social historian Callum Brown makes this statement: '...the culture of Christianity has gone in the Britain of the new millennium. Britain is showing the world how religion as we have known it can die.'[5] If by 'religion' we mean (as he does) 'religious institutions' – in particular the churches – then few of us could plausibly disagree with his claim, even if we might want to question some of the reasons that he advances to explain it.[6] Paradoxically, however, there is a growing consensus among social commentators that, at the same time as we are becoming less 'religious', we are also increasingly 'spiritual'.[7] In their book *The Experience Economy*, business strategists Joseph Pine and James Gilmour suggest that we are now leaving the visual culture behind and entering into what they call an 'immersive' culture – 'the experience economy' – in which the businesses that succeed will be the ones that can market experiences that change people's lives, 'experiences to learn and grow, develop and improve, mend and reform ... [such] transformations turn aspirants into a "new you", with all the ethical, philosophical, and religious implications that phrase implies'. In the process of explaining how they see this working, they go on to observe that 'We see people seeking spiritual growth outside the bounds of their local, traditional place of worship', which is why 'the rise of spiritual directors' can now be regarded as a business opportunity.[8]

At first glance, this might seem like a profoundly unChristian vision, until we realize that one of their key models for all this is Jesus[9] and they conclude their book with a quotation from Ephesians 2:8, and the insistence that by taking people and their needs seriously the world of business will itself undergo transformation 'because perfecting people falls under the province of God ... rather than in the domain of human business.'[10] Though we would not want to press the analogy between marketing and the Gospel too far, when we came across this book our instinctive reaction was to think, 'But isn't the church already supposed to be in the "business" that offers personal transformation?' Except, the painful truth is that the majority of people just don't see us that way. This is the dilemma of being church in an age of postmodernity, eloquently summed up by two interviewees in a survey of young adults and their spirituality published as long ago as 1994. Lisa Baker, a woman aged 20, told the interviewer that 'I honestly tried the churches, but they just couldn't speak to me ...' while Alan Bosworth (age 23) summed up his experience by saying, 'Sure, I believe in God, but I don't know what churches have to do with knowing God. It's for another time, another mindset.'[11] The same sentiments are widespread among the people of Scotland today, and not just young people. Most people are not against the church in any significant way. In fact, they rather admire and respect the valuable contributions that we have made over many generations to the life of the nation. They see us as good people, maybe even making a real difference in the world – and yet disconnected from the things that most concern them. They frequently express a sad and sincere regret that, for whatever reason, the church no longer seems to 'work' for people today in the way it apparently did for their grandparents.[12]

PRACTICAL CHALLENGES

Much has been written and said about the nature of the postmodern culture in which we now find ourselves. We do not propose to add here to the philosophical and sociological definitions of it.[13] Anyone who wants to know what we think can easily find it in other books,[14] and it is in any case subject to many different opinions. But when all the dust has settled on the arguments about what postmodernity means, we are left with three practical elements that have a direct bearing on how we might now need to redefine the church, and find new ways forward that will be both rooted in the past as well as incarnated in the present and future.

We know that things aren't working any more
We have already drawn attention to the obvious differences between

today's lifestyles and those of our grandparents. Actually, virtually nothing is exactly the same, even in everyday processes such as the way we heat our homes, wash our clothes, or prepare our food. But there are bigger changes than that, for the underlying securities of past generations have also gone. John's father worked in the electricity industry, and when he was a child he remembers him boasting to friends that nuclear energy would bring an enormous beneficial transformation to all our lives. Who would believe that today? The science and technology that once promised so much has not only failed to deliver what was hoped for, but in many instances has actually produced the opposite of that better world to which we aspire. The twentieth century was a time when we discovered the dark side of science, and realized that making a better world involves a lot more than just getting the technology right: it was the technology that made possible the mass slaughter of the First World War, of the Nazi Holocaust, the devastation of the environment, and much more besides. While no-one would wish to turn the clock back, even if it were possible, the same kind of love-hate relationship can be discerned in people's feelings about many other areas of life today, including especially institutions of all kinds (not just the churches). Whether we like it or not, we have to face realistically the fact that church life as we know it has come to be labelled as one of those things that no longer work. Taking a broader historical perspective, we can see that what has happened here was just the final nail in the coffin of that whole way of being that, in a religious setting, came to be known as 'Christendom'. The idea that there can ever be one all-embracing story that will give universal meaning to all things has been seriously undermined, if not extinguished for ever.[15]

What does all this have to do with ways of being church? In the past, because the church believed it was the repository of the only plausible 'big story' or metanarrative, our forebears were able to assume not only that they spoke on behalf of everyone, but that they had an unassailable right to speak *to* everyone. In some way or another, we were all 'Christian', because that was perceived as the only worldview that made sense of things. Some aspects of that understanding still persist, albeit in a highly attenuated and residual form, most obviously perhaps in the kind of implicit religion of those who still wish the church to be involved in their rites of passage, but who have no further interest in a living connection with the faith.[16] It also persists in some church circles.[17] Just recently, we came across a group of churches (in Scotland) that decided to address the problem of a long-term decline in membership and attendance by offering the population of its area what was described as an 'amnesty' on church membership, whereby people who had allowed their membership to 'lapse' could return on a no-questions-asked sort of basis. Such an offer would only make sense on the assumption that Christendom is still alive and well, that the church has a right to expect loyalty from the wider population, and that if we Christians can no longer engage effectively with other people, that is not our problem, but theirs. For reasons that are hard to understand, our Scottish churches seem more prone to this attitude than those in other parts of the UK.

We have a greater awareness of more of the world
Because of increased opportunities for travel, and also because the world now travels into our own homes through the medium of TV, we are much more aware of people who are different from ourselves. Whereas our grandparents might have assumed that being like them was the best way to be, and that other ways of doing things were to one degree or another 'not civilized', we can now see that things are nothing like so simple. It is perfectly possible to be a whole, fulfilled person without being 'like us'. Most of the world's people, at all times and in all places, have not been white Westerners!

In church terms, we have also become more conscious of the possibility of different ways of being church – some of which appear to be more appropriate for today's world than the ways we have inherited from our own past. The most striking example of this has to be the rapid rise of the Pentecostal movement. A hundred years ago, Pentecostal Christianity was all but non-existent: today, it is the second largest Christian grouping in the world, after the Roman Catholic tradition, and very much larger than either the Orthodox or Protestant traditions.[18] If we include the considerable numbers of people within mainline denominations worldwide who would identify themselves as 'charismatic' (as distinct from those who belong to the traditional Pentecostal denominations), the growth of this distinctive way of being church is even more dramatic still. Whether we realize it or not, we have all in one way or another been affected by this movement, if only through the many new hymns that have emerged from that tradition and which are used and enjoyed more widely – not to mention a phenomenon such as the Alpha course, which began at Holy Trinity Brompton, a charismatic Church of England congregation, and has been warmly endorsed by churches of many different outlooks. Whatever you think of it – and Alpha has its detractors as well as its enthusiasts – there is no getting away from the fact that its entire underlying philosophy is informed by a charismatic perspective. Nor can we ignore the fact that the extraordinary growth of independent charismatic churches in Britain (the New Churches) has been the one bright spot in an otherwise gloomy statistical picture over the last twenty years or so.

Yet in spite of our increasing knowledge of the wider world, and our claims to greater openness and inclusiveness, we still easily fall prey to the kind of sectarianism that bedevilled Scottish culture in past generations. Old habits die hard, and though much progress has been made, the traditional Protestant/Catholic suspicion still survives among churches today, fuelled by prejudice from both sides. More surprisingly, perhaps, is the way that a similar kind of bigotry surfaces from time to time in ecumenical circles, especially on the part of some in the mainstream establishment who speak disparagingly of others as 'fundamentalists'. When this label is applied to Pentecostals and charismatics it merely reveals the ignorance of those who use it, for whatever else they might be they emphatically cannot ever be 'fundamentalists', at least not if that term is used in its classic meaning to describe people whose sole authority is a particular understanding of the Bible. One fact alone shows that Pentecostals are hardly fundamentalists in this sense, namely that over 50% of all women who have ever been ordained in the entire history of the Church have been in Pentecostal denominations – in contrast to only 17% in major Protestant churches.[19] By definition, it is impossible to place so much emphasis on personally-received spiritual experience and be a fundamentalist. Actually, what is going on in Pentecostal theology in relation to authority and revelation is far closer to the conciliar tradition than it is even to classic Protestantism.

Neither of us would describe ourselves as either a Pentecostal or a fundamentalist – nor have we ever been – but we mention this matter here because we think it is another key area in which we need to re-examine what it means to be church in Scotland today, not least in an ecumenical context. Though we both have a fairly deep distrust of all labels, and frequently resist other people's efforts to pigeonhole us in that way, we cannot deny that we do actually belong to that liberal consensus which has dominated Scottish church life for so long. But, in different ways, we have come to realize in recent years that if our openness only extends to others who happen to be like us, then we are just kidding ourselves if we imagine that we are inclusive, or that we are reflecting the intrinsic values of the Gospel. Jesus included many strange people among his disciples, including one who would betray him and several who challenged him. Could it be that our churches are so unappealing to so many, not because of anything to do with the Gospel, but because we have become so bland – a way of being church that appeals to people like us, but which fails to speak to others who are different? Do we perhaps talk the language of inclusiveness, while all the time only engaging with other people who are like ourselves?[20] We can explore this further by moving on to the third practical consequence of postmodernity, which is . . .

We are searching for more 'spiritual' answers.

We could spend a lot of time debating what people today mean by 'spiritual' – and some Christians do. But there can be no doubt what it is that people are reacting against. In the words of sociologist George Ritzer, 'Human beings, equipped with a wide array of skills and abilities, are asked to perform a limited number of highly simplified tasks over and over. Instead of expressing their human abilities ... people are forced to deny their humanity and act in a robot-like manner. People do not express themselves ... but rather deny themselves.'[21] Transposing that into more overtly Christian language, we might say that, as people made in God's image, we are not machines but are infinitely complex individuals, of greater potential than we ever imagined. Western people as a whole are searching for new expressions of what it means to be truly human, of connecting with the Creator in ways that will not only be life-giving for ourselves, but that will empower us to make our own distinctive contribution to the well-being of the world at large, because that is a primary purpose of life. There are many things that might prevent us from achieving those aspirations, but the underlying theme is the sense of struggle and personal alienation that, in different ways, we are all wrestling with as we try to work out new ways of being in this postmodern cultural matrix.

In *The McDonaldization of the Church*, John proposed that, in missiological terms, we can identify seven people groups to whom the church must relate effectively: the desperate poor, hedonists, spiritual searchers, traditionalists, secularists, corporate achievers, and the apathetic.[22] This understanding has been widely acclaimed, and more than one reviewer has agreed with the opinion that this is 'a compelling analysis of the social and cultural groups the Churches need to reach if they are to reverse their current alarming decline',[23] which is why we introduce it here with a degree of confidence that it will be helpful as we face the task ahead. Given the fragmented nature of today's culture, a 'one size fits all' approach to church life will not be truly incarnational – if it ever was. At its best, it might be incarnational for one or two sectors of the population, and that is what we believe has happened. It is not that the Gospel has been rejected, but rather that it is not being heard because we know how to be church only for limited people groups in today's Scotland. There is nothing wrong with those people groups for whom the churches we now have are meaningful, which in turn implies that the solution to our predicament will not come through dismantling the church and starting afresh. Whatever their faults, the churches we have do clearly meet the spiritual needs of at least some people, otherwise no-one at all would be in them. But the kind of people they connect with – on this analysis, predominantly traditionalists, corporate achievers and the apathetic, to varying degrees – are the declining groups in the population, not the growing groups. What would churches for the desperate poor, or the hedonists, or the spiritual searchers look like?

LOOKING FORWARD

At last, some of you will be thinking, we are going to get some definitive statement on what 'dynamic ways of being church' might look like. In reality, though, there is unlikely to be any one simple answer to that question. For those who attend the Scottish Ecumenical Assembly in person, our contributions to the conference and reflection groups clustered around this theme will offer an opportunity to explore all that in ways that will undoubtedly be more practically oriented towards finding an answer to that key question 'how do we get from here to there?'

Rather than go down that route here, this chapter has stuck resolutely to more broadly based issues because we are convinced that we actually need to work out the answers for ourselves in relation to local circumstances. The days of what John has called the McDonaldized church are over, and if we really believe the first page of the Bible, and celebrate the fact that we are all, in our amazing diversity, people made in God's image, then that should be cause for rejoicing, not for regret. In the oft-repeated words of one of the church's most ancient liturgies, we say that worship ought to be 'for all people, at all times and in all places'. As it is, the formal worship of most of our churches is accessible only to some of the people, at very limited times and in sometimes inhospitable places. If we are to break through into dynamic ways of being church, we will need to revisit not only our understandings of what constitutes 'real' worship, but also matters connected with times and places – and to do that with integrity will in turn require us to tackle issues of power, control, money, and ultimately, theology. So what signposts would we set up as a guide to the future? In proposing a list here, we are not claiming that it is comprehensive, only that it might serve as a starting point for further discussion – and action.

First of all, it seems clear to us that we need to reaffirm the church as 'a locus of mystery', a place where God is at the centre. We do not mean to imply that God is not present everywhere (if it were not for the wider Missio Dei this entire debate would be pointless), but it is our shared conviction that, in the intellectual climate of rationalist-materialist thinking that has dominated the last few centuries of Western culture, we have somehow lost sight of the transcendent dimensions of Christian faith. The appropriate balance between beliefs and experience has been disturbed, in such a way that we have elevated theology (understood in a static way as an abstract set of rational propositions) at the expense of discipleship. In reality, you cannot have the former without the latter. Theology in its most pristine form starts with discipleship. The primary aspect of being Christian is that we are called to follow Jesus, and theology is what emerges as we reflect on the meaning of the experience. The earliest disciples appear to have followed (and, therefore, to have been 'real' disciples) long before they had any 'beliefs' about Christology, salvation, the sacraments, or indeed any of the other things we imagine to be so central to being Christian (Mark 1:16-20).[24] Moreover, the same pattern was repeated in the life of the earliest church's greatest theologian, St Paul, whose meeting with the risen Christ on the Damascus road was the source and inspiration for even his most abstract thinking, as he unpacked the significance of what had come to him first and foremost as a transcendent experience of the risen Christ.[25] It was understandable that, in the endeavour to make Christian belief more rationally accessible, our forebears should have emphasized the cognitive aspects of faith, but to be truly incarnational in today's world we ought now to be reaffirming the mysterious and transcendent aspects. Leith Anderson captures the mood of the moment when he comments that, 'The old paradigm taught that if you have the right teaching, you will experience God. The new paradigm says that if you experience God, you will have the right teaching.'[26] This is one of the points where the concerns of postmodern spiritual searchers invite us to revisit our own roots in the New Testament, and we will miss something of vital significance if we fail to do so.

A second concern that we would identify is for us to rediscover how the church can be 'a place of community', nurture, and personal growth. This also invites us to go back to our roots, while relating to one of the key concerns of contemporary culture. In a fragmented society, people are looking for a place to belong, a place of safety, a place where we can be empowered rather than stifled, and a place where we can be open with others, acknowledging our needs and inadequacies with an expectation of support rather than a fear of condemnation, and finding acceptance for who we are rather than having to conform to images of who other people think we should be.

This might be more challenging, because it will inevitably require us to value one another as persons made in God's image, regardless of class, gender, ethnicity, and other characteristics that may appear to divide us. This seems to be a particularly difficult area for the church, for as Walter Wink has eloquently reminded us, 'the vast majority of people in churches are not there to be changed but to shore themselves up against the too-rapid changes of a souped-up society.'[27] Nevertheless, it seems to us that part of being empowered for effective mission will also be the recognition that the struggle to be human, spiritual and Christian is part of life's journey, and we do not need to have our own lives in order before we can effectively witness to others. There has often been an unspoken expectation that Christian people should somehow be 'perfect', exemplified most obviously in the sort of Calvinistic ethos which has discouraged generations of believers from thinking they can ever be good enough to receive Communion. At a time when the culture generally is more tolerant of 'failure', accepting mess as part and parcel of life, should we not be encouraging one another to be true to ourselves, accepting that being Christian is not about being infallible, and that evangelism is more about inviting others to join us on the journey, because we share the same questions and problems as others have, than it is about 'selling' people the 'right' answers to life's problems?[28] Once more, the New Testament insistently calls us back to this emphasis, with many images that depict the spiritual life as a process, and its extensive use of the language of 'new birth' which also invites us to look to the future possibilities of who we might become, as distinct from the imagery of death which has been so popular with previous generations, but which inevitably directs us to the mistakes of the past, and invites us to apportion blame rather than to trust in the transforming power of God's grace.[29]

Finally (and following on from that), we need to rediscover church as 'a focus for witness and service'. Other chapters in this book relate more specifically to the prophetic role that we are called on to fulfil, so it is unnecessary to say a great deal about the nature of that role here. But what we might call our 'prophetic attitude' certainly does relate to the theme of new ways of being church, for we can only effectively challenge others to follow the way of Christ if we are continually hearing God's voice for ourselves, and allowing our lives to be challenged and changed in the process. We have something to share with others not because we are different, but because we are no different, and we can become credible witnesses not as we condemn others and dismiss what we see as their inadequate spiritualities, but as we constantly listen to the Gospel and appropriate its challenge in our own lives. 'God leaves us free to choose how to share our faith. But our options are never neutral – every methodology either illustrates or betrays the gospel we announce'.[30]

This approach will certainly be far too risky, and we have every expectation that some will regard it as too 'woolly' and maybe even dangerous. But for those who are prepared to take the risk, we believe it will hold out new possibilities of personal healing and wholeness in a fragmented world, as well as the prospect of a church renewed in its own soul. Actually (and here is a final theological point), its very weakness is likely to be the real secret of its power, and in that respect it will be incarnational in every sense of the word, for this is how Jesus himself came bearing the good news. And even St. Paul – often unfairly castigated as a revisionist commentator on the message of Jesus – reminded his readers in Corinth (who, of all people, were tempted to think that they could best do God's work in their own way and by their own power) that 'God chose what is foolish in the world to shame the wise; God chose what is weak in the world to shame the strong; God chose what is low and despised in the world, things that are not, to reduce to nothing things that are ...' (1 Corinthians 1:27-28). In our struggle to find new ways of being church in a context of rapid cultural change, that is perhaps the best news of all, and the most truly empowering message for the post-modern age.

FOR FURTHER REFLECTION

In summing all this up, here are a few further specific questions and ideas that may be especially helpful to those who will be part of the discussions on new ways of being church, at the Scottish Ecumenical Assembly.

◆ A key question that we all need to ask ourselves is, 'How inclusive do we actually want our churches to be?' To have some fun while exploring that, visit <www.belief.net> and try the quiz entitled, 'What's your Spirituality type?' that you will find there. Everyone to whom we've recommended this has found it a useful way into talking of some of these issues – and we've used it in the context of academic conferences as well as local church groups and with students. Once you've gone through it for yourself, take a look at the various categories it identifies, and reflect on the messages posted on the various bulletin boards by people who score differently. Then ask where you would like to draw the boundaries of the church, using those categories. To put it another way, what actually do you think is involved in being Christian? How much belief is enough? Or not enough?

◆ Leading on from that is a whole network of matters related to how we encounter God. This seems to be at the heart of many of the complaints about our ways of being church, heard especially from those who might be characterized as 'spiritual searchers'. We need to remember that not everybody is interested in spirituality, of course, but neither can we forget that those who are, are precisely the groups of people who, in past generations, would have been movers and shakers in the churches – and who are still active in matters related to social and personal transformation, but through other channels, most notably single-issue pressure groups. These people insistently ask us how we know that God is involved in our lives. What are we going to say to them? John Wesley famously spoke of his heart being 'strangely warmed', and in a world where people will go on to TV shows and reveal their innermost personal secrets, people want to have a blow-by-blow account of what all that means. Are we sometimes so reluctant to speak openly about our own faith and journey through life that it can seem as if we have nothing to say? This might require a major paradigm shift for some of us, because so many church people do appear to be very private individuals. What is the reason for our apparent reticence in matters of personal spirituality? And how might we encourage and stand alongside one another in an empowering way?

◆ Finally, there are several issues connected with institutional systems and organization. If we really do want church to be accessible for all people in all times and places, some things will need to change. What about those who, by definition, will never be a part of church if it only happens on Sunday mornings? This is a question whose importance is increasing at an exponential rate of growth, as we increasingly become a seven-day-a-week, 24-hours-a-day society, and as our family relationships change and reform in such a way that even for those not in work on Sundays, it is often the only day on which they can see their children, or indeed take any form of relaxation from the pressures of life — all things which, in other circumstances, Christians would tend to applaud. Are we going to be flexible enough in our approach to facilitate gatherings that can qualify as 'real church' but which may happen for some on different days and in different circumstances than has traditionally been the case? Many churches do have effective connections with their local communities, through parent and toddler groups, youth clubs, craft meetings, and whole variety of other things — and all too often bemoan the fact that the people who come on Tuesday mornings, or Wednesday lunchtimes, or Friday nights, never make it on Sundays. Do we perhaps need to think more creatively about how such activities might become spiritually meaningful in themselves, not by turning them into services, but by creating spaces in which new initiatives might spring up from those who themselves are already active in such groups? After all, that approach has been one of the most significant factors in the rapid growth of Christianity in other parts of the world. You wouldn't need to call it a 'base Christian community' to see its potential.

NOTES

CHAPTER ONE

1 See Scottish Affairs Committee, *Poverty in Scotland 1999* (House of Commons, 1999), p.xiv.

2 Aram Eisenschitz, *The View from the Grassroots* in Michael Pacione (ed), *Britain's Cities: Geographies of Division in Urban Britain* (Routledge, 1997), p156.

3 *Scottish Affairs Committee*, p.xxx.

4 See V. Elizondo & J. Sobrino (eds) *2000: Reality & Hope* (Concilium SCM Press, 1999) p111.

5 See W. Buhlmann: *With Eyes to See* (Orbis Books, 1990).

6 Elizondo *et al*, p111.

7 These stories have been compiled by Glasgow Braendam Link, a Scottish charity which works alongside people in Scotland suffering from poverty and social exclusion, committed to ensuring that the voices of the poor are listened to. Braendam Link works with ATD Fourth World, an international voluntary organisation which campaigns for human rights and supports the efforts of those in extreme poverty to take an active role in society.

8 Quoted in A. Davey, *Globalisation as Challenge and Opportunity in Urban Mission* (International Review of Mission, No. 351, 1999) p383.

9 J. Seymour (ed): *Poverty in Plenty: A Human Development Report for the UK* (Earthscan Publications, 2000) p10.

10 During the 1980s European figures show a big increase in poverty whereas in most countries it was declining. See Martin Haralambos, Martin Holborn & Robin Heald, *Sociology: Themes and Perspectives* (Collins, 2000) p311.

11 J. Seymour, p49.

12 Scottish Poverty Information Unit, *Poverty in Scotland 1999* (Glasgow Caledonian University, 1999) p41.

13 P. Alcock, *Understanding Poverty* (Macmillan, 1993) quoted in Scottish Poverty Information Unit, *Defining Poverty – October 1997* (available at http://spiu.gcal.ac.uk/briefing1.html), p1.

14 *Poverty in Scotland*, p5.

15 See C. Murray, *Underclass: The Crisis Deepens* (IEA, 1999).

16 Haralambos *et al*, p317.

17 See *Opportunity for All* (Department of Social Security, November 1999 and September 2000) and *Social Justice . . . A Scotland Where Everyone Matters* (Scottish Executive, November 1999 and September 2000).

18 According to the Scottish Foundation in evidence given to the Scottish Affairs Committee, *Poverty in Scotland*, p.xi.

19 *Social Justice 2000*.

20 Mohibur Rahman, Guy Palmer, Peter Kenway & Catherine Howarth, *Monitoring Poverty and Social Exclusion* (Joseph Rowntree Foundation, 2000), p5.

21 *Poverty in Scotland*, p6.

22 *Ibid*, p5.

23 D. Byrne, *Social Exclusion* (Open University Press, 1999), p5.

24 Scottish Affairs Committee, p.xiii.

25 *Ibid*, pxiv.

26 *Poverty in Scotland*, p9.

27 E. Graham, *Good News for the Socially Excluded? Political Theology and the Politics of New Labour* (Political Theology, Sheffield Academic Press, 2000), p77.

28 See *Speaking from Experience: Voices at the National Poverty Hearing* (CAP, 1996).

29 These are some of the testimonies of poor people gathered by Glasgow Braendam Link, used with the permission of their authors to help raise awareness of the realities of poverty in Scotland today.

30 Michael Pacione, *Urban Restructuring and the Reproduction on Inequality in Britain's Cities: An Overview* in *Britain's Cities*, p42.

31 *Defining Poverty*, p4.

32 See M. Pacione, p60.

33 *Scottish Affairs Committee*, p.xv.

34 Glasgow City Council, *Social Inclusion – Making it Happen in Scotland and Glasgow* (GDC, 2000), p18.

35 *Social Justice Annual Report 2000*, p14; 78-85.

36 *Poverty in Scotland*, p61.

37 *Social Justice 2000*, pp79-81.

38 *Ibid*, pp82-84.

39 M. Pacione, p42.

40 J. Seymour, p34.

41 M. Haralambos *et al*, p313.

42 Scottish Affairs Committee, p.xxx.

43 See, for example, *Working Together for Scotland: A Programme for Government* (Scottish Executive, 2000), Section 2.5: "We are seizing the chance to make full employment – in the modern sense of employment opportunity for all – not just a slogan but a reality for the first time in a generation."

44 J. Seymour, p85.

45 Ibid.

46 S. Craine, *The 'Black Magic Roundabout': Cyclical Social Exclusion and Alternative Careers* (1997) , quoted in M. Haralambos et al, p331.

47 *Scottish Affairs*, p.xxxix.

48 *Ibid*, p.lx.

49 *Poverty In Scotland*, p19.

50 Bob Holman, *Faith in the Poor* (Lion Books, 1998), p169.

51 *Scottish Affairs*, p.xxxvi.

52 P. Alcock, *Understanding Poverty* (Macmillan,

1997, 2nd edition) p193, quoted in M. Haralambos, p314.

[53] See T. Modood *et al*, *Ethnic Minorities in Britain: Diversity and Disadvantage* (Policy Studies Institute, 1997) in M. Haralambos et al., p313.

[54] *Poverty in Scotland*, p55.

[55] See P. Alcock.

[56] *Scottish Affairs Committee*, p.xxxi.

[57] *Poverty in Scotland*, p13.

[58] *Ibid.*

[59] See, for example, *Social Justice ... 2000*, p2.

[60] *Ibid*, p17.

[61] *Scottish Affairs Committee*, pp.xxxi-xxxii.

[62] R. Mitchell, Daniel Dorling & Mary Shaw, Inequalities in *Life & Death: What if Britain were More Equal* (Joseph Rowntree Foundation, 2000), p13.

[63] *Ibid.*

[64] *Poverty in Scotland*, p16.

[65] *Scottish Affairs Committee*, p.xxxv.

[66] *Ibid*, p.xxxiii.

[67] R. Mitchell *et al*, pp10-12.

[68] Evidence given by the Minister for Communities to the *Scottish Affairs Committee*, p.xxi.

[69] Poverty in Scotland, p69.

[70] *Ibid.*

[71] *Scottish Affairs Committee*, p.xxiii.

[72] M. Haralambos et al, p307.

[73] *What If ...?*, p48.

[74] *Ibid*, p57.

[75] *Social Justice . . . 1999*, insert (original emphasis).

[76] *Social Justice ... 2000*, p2. For a full breakdown of the targets, see *Social Justice ... A Scotland Where Everyone Matters, Milestone Sources and Definitions* (Scottish Executive, 1999), p1.

[77] *Social Justice . . . 2000*, p7.

[78] *Poverty in Scotland*, p38.

[79] David Byrne, p1.

[80] Will Hutton, *The Economics of Poverty in What If . . .?*, p22.

[81] M. Rahman *et al*, p6.

[82] *Scottish Affairs Committee*, p.xl.

[83] *Ibid*, p.xxx.

[84] *Debt on our Doorstep*, (CAP, 2000), p12.

[85] *Ibid.*

[86] *Social Justice . . . 2000*, p13.

[87] B. Holman, *A Voice from the Estate in Elaine Graham*, p93.

[88] Jane Tewson, *A New Sort of Charity in What If . . .?*, p106.

[89] Matthew 25:31-46.

[90] *Scottish Affairs Committee*, p.xxviii.

[91] Luke 4:18.

[92] E. Graham, p91.

[93] Rose Wu, Standing with the Poor or the Powerful?, (International Review of Mission, vol.87, 1998), p217.

[94] V. Jones, A Future in Community in Changing the Agenda: Christian Reflections on Mission and Community Work (BCC, 1989), p55.

CHAPTER TWO

[1] *The Democratic Intellect: Scotland and her universities in the nineteenth century*, (Edinburgh University Press) c.1961.

[2] Keynote address, CEM Conference, Edinburgh 1995: 'Educational Values and the Money Culture.'

[3] Ibid.

CHAPTER THREE

[1] A number of people have challenged the categories that GROS has decided to use for ethnic classification in Census 2001 Scotland. The categories are confusing as they use a mixture of ethnicity, colour, nationality, and furthermore define Africans in terms of what they are and not by who they are.

[2] Women's organisations in the UK and Africa have organised campaigns and information sessions to stop bleaching.

[3] The next UN World Conference on Racism will take place in Durban, South Africa, in August 2001.

[4] People of concern to UNHCR include: refugees, internally displaced people, asylum seekers and those who have returned.

[5] Richard Jolly comments in the UN report about the increase in poverty in the world. *Guardian* July 1999 article by Charlotte Denny and Victoria Britain.

[6] Existing Instruments and Conventions
UK
Race Relations Act 1976
Race Relations Amendments 2000
Stephen Lawrence inquiry Report Recommendations 1999
International
UN Universal Declaration of Human Rights 1948
UN International Convention on the Elimination of all forms of Racial Discrimination Dec.1965
International Covenant on Civil and Political Rights 1976
International Covenant on Economic Social and Cultural Rights 1976
Convention on the Elimination of Discrimination against Women (CEDAW) 1979
International Convention on the Protection of Migrant Workers and Members of Families 1990
Global Platform for Action Beijing 1995
European
European Convention on the Protection of Human Rights and Fundamental Freedoms 1950
European Convention on the Legal Status of Migrant Workers 1983
European Social Chapter 1965 (Maastricht European Council 1991)
European Convention of Human Rights

Vienna Declaration 1993
1997 – European Year Against Racism and Xenophobia
European Directives on Prevention of Racism and Xenophobia – Article 13, Nov.1999.

[7] *A few years ago, I went to Australia on a land rights solidarity visit to the Aboriginal People. At one of the many gatherings a group of children came to sit beside me and like children all over the world, they found something more interesting to do than listen to long speeches. They giggled when they noticed a few people falling asleep, overcome by heat and tiredness. They turned to me. A few of them touched my hand as if they were examining something. They became more excited and whispered to each other and more of them came closer and rubbed my arm. This behaviour puzzled me because their skin was the same as mine, if not a shade darker. One of them told me that I was different because I had no hair on my arms and legs. I promptly rubbed some red soil on my arms to make the fine hair on my skin visible and then we all laughed together. I was the first African they had even seen. Their inquisitive nature, their curiosity and ability to notice the difference, was identical to that of white children in a nursery school who were fascinated by my colour and my hair when I took my children to the school.*

SOURCES:

Larsen, Nella, *Quicksand and Passing*, Rutgers University Press, 1986, New Jersey.
McDowell, D. E, ed. Serpents Tail, 1989, London.
McPherson, Sir William, *Stephen Lawrence Inquiry Report*, Home Office, Feb 1999
Echoes Issue, 17/200, *Today's Face of Racism*, WCC Publication, Geneva, 2000
Usha Brown 1998: 'The nature of Racism in Britain in the 1990s' in the *Communities against Racism Conference Report* – 1997
Parekh Report, *The Future of Multi-ethnic Britain*, Profile Books Ltd, London, 2000
Futures of Refugees and Refugee Settlement, International Catholic Migration (ICMC), May 2000
CCRJ, *A Christian Response to Racism, Report and Action for the Churches*, London
Steve Cohen: *Imagine There's No Countries —1992 and international immigration controls against migrants, immigrants and refugees*
New Internationalist No 286, Sept.1996
New Routes, A journal of peace Research and Action, Special issue, Vol.3, no 1, 1998
World Refugee Survey 1995 and 1996
Mama, A 1989 *The Hidden Struggle*
New Internationalist, 1989 'Women: A World Report'
White, E. C. Ed 1990 *Black Women's Health Book* Report of the European Working Conference

CHAPTER FOUR

[1] The references to the Bible use the standard abbreviations for identification of the books concerned

[2] Second Vatican Ecumenical Council, Pastoral Constitution on the Church in the Modern World (Gaudium et spes) no38 (1966) p1055

[3] Encyclical letter of Pope John Paul II on Human Work (Laborem Exercens) section 6

[4] The author's lack of experience necessarily restricts this review to a focus on the United Kingdom, drawing on literature primarily from Europe and the United States. It is readily acknowledged that the experience of work in other world contexts will be radically different. The author is however seeking to address issues for an audience in Scotland, but recognises without question that the local situation cannot be abstracted from the global.

[5] Source: Employment Gazette

[6] Source: Ceridian Performance Partners

[7] Employment Gazette Historical Supplement October 1994

[8] A Christensen (1983) *Lönearebeitet some samhällsform och ideology* Sekretariat för framtidstudier

[9] J Finch (1989) *Family Obligations and Social Change* Cambridge: Polity

[10] It is no longer the case that women with dependent children are less likely to be in paid employment than other women. A major shift has been in the percentage of women with children under 5 years who are now in work which has moved from about a quarter in the early 1970s to about a half now

[11] GL Staines and J Pleck (1983) *The Impact of work schedules on the family* Ann Arbor: University of Michigan Survely Research Center Elder care is primarily undertaken by women, even where the dependent elder is the parent of the male partner, ie the carers are principally daughters and daughters-in-law.

[12] J Pleck (1989) *Family Supportive Employer Policies and Man's Participation* Washington DC: National Research Council; H Wilkinson (1994) *No turning back: Generations and the Genderquake* London: Demos

[13] HB Presser (1989) 'Can we make time for children?' *Demography* 26 (4) pp523-543

[14] Source: Equal Opportunities Commission

[15] The teaching profession is perhaps amongst the most evident. Where there is now greater gender equality amongst entrants, eg to branches of the legal profession, there remains little evidence of access to the "top" appointments, though some would argue that it will take some time for the new entrants to reach the "qualifying" stage in their professional life. See, for example, D Berry-Lound (1990) *Work and the Family* London: (the then) Institute of Personnel Management (now the Chartered Institute of Personnel and Development)

[16] See Christensen (1983) on the issue of how far women choose this form of employment and

on whether they would make such a choice if, for example, suitable child care or flexible working arrangements were in place to allow them to take up full-time employment

[17] Gertrude Williams (1945) *Women and Work* London: Nicholson and Watson

[18] Speech by Margaret Hodge, Minister for Employment and Equal Opportunities, DfEE

[19] J Pullinger and C Summerfield (1998) *Social Focus on Women and Men* London: HMSO

[20] G Dench (1996) *Transforming Men: changing patterns of dependency and dominance in gender relations* New Brunswick, NJ: Transaction Publishers

[21] J Warin, Y Solomon, C Lewis and W Langford (1999) *Fathers, work and family life* Family Policy Studies Centre and Joseph Rowntree Foundation

[22] S Middleton, K Ashworth and R Walker (1994) *Family Fortunes: pressures on parents and children in the 1990s* London: Child Poverty Action Group

[23] The expression work-life balance is perhaps an unfortunate one, as it might seem to suggest that work is not part of life, whereas it is an integral and essential element of living. Nonetheless, it is the generally accepted "official" term for this balance of life within paid work and life outwith paid work.

[24] E Galinsky and PJ Stein (1990) 'The Impact of human resource policies on employees balancing work/family life' *Jnl of Family Issues* 11(4) pp3689-383

[25] AT&T

[26] C Glynn (1999) *Enabling Balance: The Importance of Organisational Culture* Roffey Park Management Institute

[27] The same survey suggested that respondents were much more able to keep home issues out of work. A degree of caution has to be exercised in relation to such surveys which depend significantly on respondent's self-report, however

[28] References to families are not intended to be read narrowly and the writer would wish to acknowledge that there is considerable diversity in what constitute "families" including lone parent or same sex parenting families

[29] Eg onsite day centres for pre-school and school children, parental leave arrangements, job protection schemes, part-time working arrangements for returning parents, flexitime, working at home, family sick days, unpaid leave. See BW MacLennan (1992) 'Stressor reduction: an organizational alternative to individual stress management' in JC Quick, LT Murphy and JJ Hurrell (eds) *Stress and Well-being at Work: Assessments and Interventions for Occupational Mental Health* Washington DC: American Psychological Association

[30] Institute for Personnel and Development *Living to Work*

[31] Institute for Employment Research of the University of Warwick and IFF Research

[32] Japan Ministry of Labour, Tokyo 27 June 2000

[33] BBC online network news 2 September 1999

[34] European Foundation for the Improvement of Living and Working Conditions (1998) *Labour Market Participation: Now and in the future* Dublin

[35] Occupational and Environmental Medicine (2000) no 57 pp649-55

[36] University of Science and Technology in Manchester

[37] E Rotheiler, P Richter, M Rudolf and JW Hinton (1997) 'Further cross-cultural factor validation on the FABA self report inventory of coronary-prone behaviours' *Psychology and health* 12, 505-12

[38] A Uris (1972) 'How managers ease job pressures' *International Management* June pp 45-46

[39] L Breslow and P Buell (1960) ' Mortality from coronary heart disease and physical activity of work in California' *Jnl of Chronic Diseases* 22, 87-91

[40] HI Russek and BL Zohman (1958) 'Relative significance of heredity, diet and occupational stress in CHD of young adults' *American Jnl of Medical Sciences* 235, 266-275

[41] European Foundation for Living and Working Conditions (1996) *Working Conditions report*

[42] See, for example, T Cox and CJ Mackay (1981) 'A transactional approach to occupational stress' in EN Corlett and J Richardson (eds) *Stress, Work design and Productivity* Chichester: Wiley and Sons

[43] A Windel and B Zimolong (1997) 'Group work and performance in business' *Gruppendynamik-Zeitscchrift for Angewandte Sozialpsychologie* 28(4) pp333-5

[44] JRP French, W Rogers and S Cobb (1982) 'A model of person-environment fit' in GW Coehlo, DA Hamburg and JE Adams (eds) *Coping and Adaptation* New York: Basic Books

[45] H Selye (1956) *Stress of Life* New York: McGraw Hill

[46] Health and Safety Executive statistics

[47] J Kearns (1986) 'Stress at work: the challenge of change' *The Management of Health* 1 Stress and the City BUPA

[48] LR Murphy, JJ Hurrell and JC Quick (1992) 'Work and well-being: where do we go from here?' in JC Quick, LR Murphy and JJ Hurrell (eds) *Stress and well-being at work* Washington DC: American Psychological Association

CHAPTER SIX

[1] B. Moore, *Reflections on the Causes of Human Misery*, (Allen Lane Penguin Press, London, 1972) p. 193.

[2] K. Popper, *Conjectures and Refutations*, (Routledge and Kegan Paul, London, 1969).

[3] K. Popper, *op. cit.*, p. 153.

[4] E. Durkheim, *The Elementary Forms of Religious*

Life, (Free Press, New York, 1995) p. 239.

5 P. Berger and T. Luckmann, *The Social Construction of Reality,* (Allen Lane Penguin Press, London, 1966).

6 P. Berger, *The Social Reality of Religion,* (Faber and Faber, London, 1969).

7 H. Collins and T. Pinch, *Frames of Meaning: The Social Construction of Extraordinary Science,* (Routledge and Kegan Paul, London 1982.

8 I. Hacking, *The Social Construction of What?* (Harvard University Press, London, 1999).

9 D. MacKenzie and J. Wajcman, eds., *The Social Shaping of Technology,* (Open University Press, Buckingham, 1999) p. 7.

10 Z. Bauman, *Modernity and the Holocaust,* (Policy, Oxford, 1989) p. x.

11 *Ibid,* p. 27.

12 H. Marcuse, *Industrialisation and Capitalism,* in O. Stammer, ed., *Max Weber and Sociology Today,* (Blackwell, Oxford, 1971) p. 149.

13 U. Beck, *Risk Society: Towards a New Modernity,* (Sage, London, 1992); U. Beck, *Ecological Politics in an Age of Risk,* (Polity, Oxford, 1995); U. Beck, *World Risk, Society,* (Polity, Oxford, 1999).

14 U. Beck, (1999) p. 152.

15 A. Giddens, *Modernity and Self-Identity,* (Polity, Oxford, 1991) p. 124.

16 U. Beck, (1995) p.36.

17 D. Haraway, *Modest Witness @ Second Millennium,* in MacKenzie and Wajcman *op.cit.* p. 47.

18 *The Guardian,* (12 February 2001) p. 7.

19 R. Ferguson, Technology at the Crossroads. The Story of the Society, Religion and Technology Project), St Andrew Press, Edinburgh, 1994) p. 14.

20 *Ibid,* p. 15.

21 H. Davis, ed., Ethics and Defence, Power and Responsibility in the Nuclear Age, (Blackwell, Oxford, 1986).

22 D. Bruce and A. Bruce eds., Engineering Genesis, The Ethics of Genetic Engineering in Non-Human Species, Earthscan, London, 1998).

23 R. Ferguson, *op.cit.,* p. xi.

24 Society, Religion and Technology Project, *While the Earth Endures,* (SRT, Edinburgh, 1986).

25 Cited in R. Ferguson, *op.cit.,* pp. 71-2.

26 *Ibid,* p. 74.

27 E. Hobsbawn, *The New Century,* (Abacus, London, 2000) pp. 166-7.

CHAPTER SEVEN

1 For a recent analysis of the spiritual state of Britain in the light of the secularization thesis, see Steve Bruce, *Religion in Modern Britain* (Oxford: Oxford University Press 1995). A different account, questioning the secularization thesis, is in Grace Davie, *Religion in Britain since 1945* (Oxford: Blackwell 1994).

2 For a succinct account of the changes, see Diana Gittins, *The Family in Question* (London: Macmillan 1993, 2nd ed); and for a Christian perspective, John Drane & Olive M Fleming Drane, *Happy Families?* (London: HarperCollins 1995); Herbert Anderson, Don Browning, et al, *The Family Handbook* (Louisville KY: Westminster John Knox Press 1998).

3 For convenient summaries of recent statistical trends, see Peter Brierley *Religious Trends 2000/2001* (London: Christian Research 2000).

4 David B Barrett, George T Kurian, & Todd M Johnson (eds), *World Christian Encyclopedia: a Comparative Survey of Churches and Religions in the Modern World* (New York: Oxford University Press 2001, 2nd ed. in 2 volumes).

5 Callum Brown, *The Death of Christian Britain* (London: Routledge 2001), 198.

6 For a corrective, from a world perspective, see Peter Berger (ed), *The Desecularization of the World* (Grand Rapids: Eerdmans 1999).

7 For an account of this geared to the American situation, but not wholly irrelevant to Britain, see Wade Clark Roof, *Spiritual Marketplace* (Princeton: Princeton University Press 1999); and on the spirituality of young people, Tom Beaudoin, *Virtual Faith: the irreverent spiritual quest of Generation X* (San Francisco: Jossey Bass 1998).

8 B Joseph Pine & James H Gilmore, *The Experience Economy* (Boston: Harvard Business School Press 1999). The quotations here are all from chapter 9 (163-164, 183). This is by no means the only management text to use Biblical concepts in this way: cf also Laurie Beth Jones, *Jesus CEO: using ancient wisdom for visionary leadership* (New York: Hyperion 1995).

9 *The Experience Economy,* 182-183.

10 The Experience Economy, 206.

11 George Barna, *Baby Busters* (Chicago: Northfield 1994), 93, 143-144.

12 For a succinct account of all this, see Paul Vallely, 'Evangelism in a Post-Religious Society', in *Setting the Agenda: the Report of the 1999 Church of England Conference on Evangelism* (London: Church House Publishing 1999), 30-43.

13 For useful treatments of postmodernity in relation to theology and church life, see David Lyon, *Postmodernity* (Buckingham: Open University Press 1994); David S Dockery, *The Challenge of Postmodernism* (Wheaton IL: Bridgepoint 1995); and for a penetrating critique of the dominant Western understanding of postmodernity as a liberating philosophy, Ziauddin Sardar, *Postmodernism and the Other* (London: Pluto Press 1998).

14 John Drane & Olive M Fleming Drane, *Happy Families?* (London: HarperCollins 1995); John Drane, *Cultural Change and Biblical Faith* (Carlisle: Paternoster Press 2000); *The McDonaldization of the Church* (London:

Darton Longman and Todd 2000); Olive M Fleming Drane, *Clowns, Storytellers and Disciples* (Oxford: BRF, forthcoming).

[15] Most famously expressed by Jean-François Lyotard, who defined postmodernity at its simplest as 'incredulity toward metanarratives', *The Postmodern Condition* (Minneapolis: University of Minnesota Press 1993), xxiv.

[16] On implicit religion more generally, see Edward I Bailey, *Implicit Religion: an Introduction* (London: Middlesex University Press 1998).

[17] Much as we would like to agree with William Storrar's belief that the church 'married modernity ... [only] for the best of missiological reasons', there is just a bit too much evidence that seems to suggest that some church people have gone well beyond that, and actually enjoy the status and perceived social standing that embracing Christendom-style attitudes to culture gives them. Cf W F Storrar, 'From Braveheart to Faint-heart: worship and culture in postmodern Scotland', in B D Spinks & I R Torrance (eds), *To Glorify God: Essays on Modern Reformed Liturgy*(Edinburgh: T & T Clark 1999), 78; and John Drane, *Cultural Change and Biblical Faith*, 112-116.

[18] According to Walter J Hollenweger, *Pentecostalism: Origins and Developments Worldwide* (Peabody MA: Hendrickson 1997), 1, the rapid expansion of Pentecostalism represents 'a growth which is unique in church history, not excluding the early centuries of the church'. For more on the phenomenon, see also Murray W Dempster, Byron D Klaus, & Douglas Petersen (eds), *The Globalization of Pentecostalism* (Oxford: Regnum 1999).

[19] See Barbara Brown Zikmund, 'Women and Ordination', in Rosemary Radford Ruether & Rosemary Skinner Keller (eds), *In Our Own Voices: Four Centuries of American Women's Religious Writing* (San Francisco: HarperCollins 1995), 299

[20] We realize that this may sound like a counsel of perfection, and that of course a dialogue needs to take place in two directions. In the Scottish context, Christian groups that have not previously operated in the context of formal ecumenical structures are likely to be somewhat wary of our intentions, often for good reasons. However, there is a very obvious contrast here between Scottish attitudes and those which prevail in England, where strenuous efforts have been made to be more inclusive, and have in some instances led to an infusion of new life and energy into ecumenical life, not least through the involvement of leaders from the New Churches. In some respects this was probably made easier by the existence of strong black-led churches in England, which presented a particular moral challenge to the mainline denominations, for they only came into existence as a consequence of the racism of English churches in the 1950s and 1960s. Nonetheless, despite the different cultural baggage, we remain convinced that similar overtures to such groups in Scotland could make a real difference to the overall energy levels of Scottish Christianity, and would make a much more significant contribution to the re-evangelization of Scotland than moves towards organic union of a limited number of churches, which we regard as an agenda for the past rather than for the future.

[21] George Ritzer, *The McDonaldization of Society* (Thousand Oaks CA: Pine Forge Press 1993), 26.

[22] *The McDonaldization of the Church* 55-84.

[23] John Wolffe, in *Church Times* 9 March 2001, 16.

[24] Cf John Drane, *Faith in a Changing Culture* (London: HarperCollins 1997), 218-223; Richard V Peace, *Conversion in the New Testament* (Grand Rapids: Eerdmans 1999).

[25] See Seyoon Kim, *The Origin of Paul's Gospel* (Grand Rapids: Eerdmans 1984).

[26] Leith Anderson, *A Church for the Twenty-First Century* (Minneapolis: Bethany House 1992), 21.

[27] Walter Wink, *Transforming Bible Study* (Nashville: Abingdon Press 1990), 69.

[28] For a Biblically-based exploration of this understanding of Christian life, see Janet O. Hagberg & Robert A. Guelich, *The Critical Journey* (Salem WI: Sheffield Publishing Co. 1995).

[29] Historically, this phenomenon is connected with the male dominance of theology. Cf John Drane, *The McDonaldization of the Church*, 173-182; Grace Jantzen, 'Necrophilia and Natality: what does it mean to be religious?' in *Scottish Journal of Religious Studies* 19/1 (1998), 101-121; Margaret L Hammer, *Giving Birth: Reclaiming Biblical Metaphor for Pastoral Practice* (Louisville: Westminster John Knox Press 1994).

[30] *Mission and Evangelism, an Ecumenical Affirmation* (Geneva: World Council of Churches 1982), paragraph 28.